The enchanted heemparks of Amstelveen

The enchanted heemparks of Amstelveen

A walk through the heemparks
De Braak, Dr. Koos Landwehrpark
and Dr. Jac. P. Thijssepark

Ariën Slagt
Arlette Kouwenhoven

LM Publishers

Contents

Foreword   5

Wonder, daydream and enjoy   6

De Braak   8

Dr. Koos Landwehrpark   48

Dr. Jac. P. Thijssepark   56

List of plant names   120

Foreword

The borough of Amstelveen is frequently praised for its beautiful green areas, and our beautiful parks with indigenous plants are one of the main reasons for these tributes.

Of course, our greenery can be enjoyed by simply walking in the idyllic parks, but I believe this enjoyment is enhanced by knowing what you are looking at. I am therefore extremely pleased by the publication of this booklet.

Using this booklet as your guide while you stroll along the paths will bring you closer to the history of these beautiful heemparks. You will also find a wealth of information about the trees and plants you encounter.

And remember, while you read the fascinating information in this guide, don't forget to look around you every few sentences. It would be a pity if you acquire a great deal of knowledge during your walk, while the beauty of the parks eludes you...

I sincerely wish you many pleasant strolls in Amstelveen's heemparks – they are always beautiful, regardless of the season.

JAN VAN ZANEN,
Mayor of Amstelveen

Wander, daydream and enjoy

'He doesn't know the names of everything that grows there, but he recognises many familiar shapes and senses the murmuring of something he once experienced but cannot put into words. He recognises the Black Elderberry, the Hawthorn, the Ragged Robin and the Ox-eye Daisy from his youth, from a solitary stroll on a summer morning. It felt as if he was donning an old, well-worn coat that he always felt so good in, because it was such a comfortable fit: now he regretted throwing that coat away.'

Thus did Koos Landwehr, one of the founders of parks dedicated to indigenous ('heem') plants in the Netherlands, describe in simple yet striking language the essence of what he meant by a 'heempark'. Of course, people can relax here in tranquil surroundings that allow them to forget the world outside for a moment and recharge their batteries. School children learn about the enormous diversity of flora in the Netherlands and how important it is to manage it carefully. But it is exactly those melancholic ripples that pass through you as you follow the winding paths and see the shades of white, yellow and purple, and the delicate flowers swaying and bobbing in the breeze, and smell their fragrances that, more than anything else, remind you of the past: this is 'heem', this is 'home', and it is especially this

View over the large lake in the Jac. P. Thijssepark

that Landwehr and the other founders of the heemparks in Amstelveen envisaged.

Regardless of whether you have only a moment or an ocean of time we would like to invite you to stroll through De Braak, the Dr. Jac. P. Thijssepark and the Dr. Koos Landwehrpark – with this book in hand – and take you to that wonderful place called 'home'. They still grow here, the plants of yore: Cornflowers, Upland Enchanter's Nightshade and Scottish Harebells, even if they are no longer profuse in fields, or alongside roads and ditches. Decades of ceaseless construction and changes to land management and agricultural techniques have resulted in some varieties such as Wood Buttercup and Dwarf Cornel becoming extinct or hardly ever growing in the wild. Other varieties such as Common Butterwort and Marsh St. John's Wort have been saved from extinction, but they are nowhere near as widespread as they once were in swamps or bodies of water. All these plants have their place in Amstelveen's heemparks that cover an area of approximately 11 hectares, be it in the open compositions of bodies of water and surrounding greenery in De Braak, in the romantic and more enclosed 'garden rooms' in the Dr. Jac P. Thijssepark, or in the rugged Molinia meadow in the Dr. Koos Landwehrpark. We invite you to wander, daydream and get lost in the colours, fragrances and forms of our enchanting indigenous flora, no matter the season.

De Braak

Our stroll starts at the entrance to De Braak because this was
the first of Amstelveen's three heemparks to be laid out. Pause
for a moment for a smattering of history that will enhance your
understanding of why this park is what it is. In 1939, an old
peat lake called De Braak was part of an ambitious project that
the Nieuwer-Amstel municipality, of which Amstelveen village
was a part, hoped would draw well-to-do commuters from
Amsterdam by creating greener surroundings. This was in

View over Het Eiland and the Drijvend Pad

reaction to the annexation of large swathes of the Nieuwer-Amstelse territory by the city of Amsterdam in 1896 and 1921, which threatened to return the borough to the agrarian community it had been for centuries.

The Nieuwer-Amstelse municipality's plans in the 1920s prioritised urban greenery and scenic beauty. In 1926 landscape architect Dirk Frederik Tersteeg (1876–1942) was appointed and realised the first project, named the Wandelpark ('Walking Park'). This park would later be named after Chris Broerse, the head gardener appointed in 1927. Luxury houses

When these three heemparks were constructed, the term 'heempark' was not yet in use. It was only in 1946 that Chris Broerse proposed using it in the specialist journal *De Boomkwekerij* ('The Tree Nursery') for gardens, parks and public spaces with wild plants. He chose the term along with the then-town clerk H.J. Scharp, who besides being a public servant, was also a historian and coin collector. The term 'heempark' is derived from older words such as 'heemkunde', which refer to the study of local history and geography. Broerse described it as follows: 'People should feel as if they are surrounded by distinctive aspects of their living environment, by the soil and climate they know and trust. Then they will feel at home surrounded by the vegetation, birds and butterflies from their own countryside, where even the drifting cloud banks are reassuring; being "at home", is, in other words, "not feeling out of place."' Landwehr distinguished between later heemparks in a limited sense, such as the parks described here, and in the broadest sense. The latter include old city and landscape elements such as ramparts, wooden banks, mud banks or sandbanks, dykes, verges and suchlike. Landwehr: 'The created landscape had to appear to have always been there, the difference being that is can actually be experienced'.
Moreover, it must be pointed out that 'inheems' or 'indigenous to the Netherlands' are relative terms, because they are applied to plants that have grown here for at least 100 years. You will notice that a number of plants in the heemparks are classified as indigenous despite travelling here from far-flung quarters of the world in the distant past.

and villas in the north-west of the borough would be swathed in green. The neighbourhood bordered the Amsterdamse Bos, a 1000-hectare landscape park constructed during the crisis years of the 1930s as a relief work project. The parks adjacent to it, including De Braak, would also take shape more rapidly for the same reason. Existing ponds and lakes, the ring canals in the various polders, the Poel, the Landscheidingsvaart and the Hoornsloot, would remain virtually unchanged in the design so as to retain a historic link between the new plans and the area's nineteenth-century landscape.

The old peat lake De Braak originated in the seventeenth century with the collapse of a section of the dike around the lake Haarlemmermeer. The peat was soggy and nutrient-poor, making it unsuitable for the usual cultivated plants. Inspired by publications about the use of wild plants elsewhere in

Europe, and especially by his experiences while constructing a 'natural garden' in Berlin, Broerse decided to work with wild plants, which he cultivated according to plant sociological principles, i.e., taking into account the various mutual relations and interdependencies. He soon realised that this approach did not work in the context of a small park. Some varieties hardly grew at all, while others could only be restrained with considerable effort. 'Plant communities cannot be imitated; they arise through conditions that to some degree are beyond human control', wrote Broerse later. He therefore modified the swamp forest he originally envisaged by using an artificially assembled community of plants that had the shared characteristic of all being indigenous. He planted Alder, Willow, Birch, Oak and Alder Buckthorn and introduced colour with Dog Rose, Guelder-Rose and undervalued herbs such as Lesser Celandine, Marsh Thistle and Devil's-bit Scabious. With this approach he developed a way to concentrate and create a park from the natural and semi-natural landscapes he knew so well.
He decided to call these green areas 'heemparks', which are,

De Doorbraak, with view over the exotic corner

Chris Broerse was born on 7 September 1902 in Serooskerke on Walcheren, a former island in Zeeland province, the Netherlands. Like his father before him, he was meant to be a house painter, but this held no appeal. His forays around the island ignited his passion for nature. He wanted to work with plants, and even threatened to leave home if denied his dream. His stubborn-ness paid off and at the age of 11 he began working in the local vegetable garden. Later he worked at a country estate near Eindhoven, where he met landscape architect Tersteeg, who did a lot of work for Amstelveen municipality. It was through Tersteeg that Broerse received a 25-year appointment as head of the municipality's green areas. Tersteeg's lessons, a lot of focused study and his own

Chris P. Broerse, 1941

phenomenal insight led to Broerse rapidly being appointed director of Amstelveen's Parks and Public Gardens Department and of Zorgvlied cemetery on the Amstel River. Broerse created the 'heempark' phenomenon with De Braak and the Dr. Jac. P. Thijssepark in Amstelveen. By focusing on heemparks he promoted the use of indigenous plants in our country. Broerse did not only design public green spaces; among others, he was also responsible for the design of the Free University's Botanical Garden in Amsterdam; the renovation of Landgoed Drakensteijn, a castle and rural estate in Soest; and a number of office gardens. He also had a pivotal influence on the look of the famous Zorgvlied cemetery. Broerse was a versatile man, with a determination that some occasionally found confrontational. As chairman of the Bond van Nederlandse Tuinarchitecten (Association of Netherlands Landscape Gardeners) and a columnist in specialist journals, his many suggestions stimulated discussions and exchanges in his field. He resigned as director in Amstelveen in 1967. It was on his resignation that the Wandelpark, designed by Tersteeg, was named after him. Nine years later he was awarded the J.T.P. Bijhouwerprijs for garden and landscape architecture. Chris P. Broerse died in 1995 at the age of 92. To a large extent he determined the appearance of Amstelveen's green belt.

in effect, an Amstelveen invention. Broerse used plants from the Netherlands to create picturesque views that appealed to the eye. Every view and perspective had to look like a painting. What Broerse envisioned is apparent to anyone entering De Braak: an architectonically pure, balanced composition with its own distinct character that could not be affected by the dynamics of the individual plant types, a character that is determined by large bodies of water combined with reed lands, patches of dense forest and quite large areas of heathland.

The **Kwekerijpad** – your starting point – not only provides a beautiful preview of the vistas in this park, but it also allows you to take a look at the municipal heemplant nursery (Kwekerij) about 50 metres along on your left. While preparing De Braak it was assumed that accessing heemplants would be simpler than it was in reality. Not a single nursery could supply the required plants. So a nursery was constructed in the north-western corner of the park, with the aforementioned Koos Landwehr as supervisor. Landwehr travelled throughout the Netherlands in his little Renault car, collecting thousands of plants, seeds and cuttings. While knowledge about cultivation techniques for many varieties was scant, he nonetheless succeeded by accident or design to breed many varieties. Of course, the varieties that grow naturally in peat were the most successful, and after experimenting, selecting and giving plants time to adapt to

Yellow Camomile and Long-leaf Speedwell

Plant sociology

When Chris Broerse began designing the De Braak heempark, he wanted to reproduce plant communities exactly, but on a smaller scale. At the time there were no standard works about plant communities in the Netherlands. E. Meyer Drees had written the book *De Bosvegetatie van de Achterhoek en enkele aangrenzende gebieden* ('Forest Vegetation in the Achterhoek and Several Adjoining Areas') in 1936, a work Broerse consulted constantly. In 1940 Victor Westhoff and J. Meltzer wrote the book *Inleiding tot de Plantensociologie* ('Introduction to Plant Sociology'), and a year later, with J.W. Dijk, *Overzicht van de Plantengemeenschappen in Nederland* ('Compendium of Plant Communities in the Netherlands'). Broerse made full use of the information in these books from the moment he acquired them.

Why do certain plants grow together in communities? It has to do with the partiality of plants for the places where they grow. The amount of nourishment, water and light and, for example, the salt or zinc values in the soil can play a decisive role in why plants root and flourish in certain locations. This is not to say that a particular plant would not grow without salt or zinc, but rather that it has a higher tolerance to higher quantities of either, while many other plants do not, which gives it an advantage. Plants that grow in the same conditions or are complementary in some way (for example, trees and shade-loving varieties) frequently form communities. Within such plant communities some varieties are less prevalent than the others. Some varieties will always be present; others often only have a single representative. This is not always due to natural causes. Human intervention over centuries has left its mark. If a parcel of land is ploughed and seeded with grain year after year, it will eventually result in a plant community that can survive in these manipulated conditions, a community that largely consists of annuals (see the section on cornfield flowers on pp. 102–3).

In plant sociology, communities are categorised according to a system that can be compared to the way plants are classified. They are called 'associations', consisting of one or more leading plant species and one or more accompanying plants. These associations are again divided into sub-associations, varieties and sub-varieties, similar to families of plants, gender, type and sub-types. They have a common name and a scientific name. For example, a mixed Oak-Hornbeam forest has the scientific name *Querceto-Carpinetum stachyetosum*.

Broerse was unable to fulfil his hope of reproducing and combining plant communities on a smaller scale. He could not explain this, but nonetheless

View of the pool in De Braak from the Van Leerpad with Bog-rosemary and Creeping Willow in the foreground

continued to incorporate plant sociology in his designs. When designing wooded areas in De Braak he especially focused on Alder, Birch, Willow and Oak-Hornbeam forests. Many trees in these woods have died or fallen down in recent decades. We try to replace them with trees of the same type or at least from the same community. Following Broerse, we weigh up the aesthetic effects of various combinations, and sometimes other varieties are chosen. This is because it would be strange to allow varieties that are very rare in the wild or have even disappeared from our country, for example, Ivy-leaved Bellflower, Bog Asphodel and Great Horsetail, to dominate in the parks. Once you realise that ten people are busy every day weeding out unwanted varieties, it enhances your appreciation of the subtlety of plant ecologies. Plants that would otherwise be dominant – grasses, for example – are removed so that varieties that would otherwise be squeezed out in the wild can replace them, thereby becoming more prevalent.

these conditions, he even managed to cultivate alkali-loving varieties on peat.

We only work with plants that are 100 per cent indigenous or pure strains of 'stinsplants' (exotic species that primarily grow on homesteads and which have gone wild, see the section on stinsplants on p. 104). Breeding the plants ourselves guarantees the purity of the strains. In the past 70 years tens of thousands of plants in the heemparks and in the green areas with heemplants in Amstelveen and its environs began their lives in this nursery. Even the forest, Amsterdamse Bos, is speckled with heemplants, many of which are from our heemplant nursery. Specific varieties are cultivated on different types of soil; currently, this is done to replace dead plants. All varieties that are easy to grow from cuttings but which are highly labour intensive and take a lot of room such as Cowberry are outsourced piecemeal to professional plant cuttings companies.

Equally labour intensive, but work we do ourselves, is maintaining the trees and shrubs that sometimes take years to shape at the nursery to use as individuals or in groups to create

Wall flora

Basins, with herbs and grains in the background

a particular view: you will encounter birch trees with multiple trunks that are bent in unusual ways in the park.

The wall made of slate and roofing tiles near the ditch at the rear of the nursery was erected to display the Netherlands' wall plants. Because of their specific requirements these delicate varieties cannot be planted in the heemparks.

Each of the small and large round basins sustains a unique micro-environment, from lime-rich and dry to acidic and wet. The basins are arranged as a series: there is a terrestialisation series, a dune series, a high moorland series, basins in a pioneering phase, and a calcareous grassland series. Great care is taken with these basins. The water level is artificially maintained, they are protected from frost, and undesirable varieties are weeded out. This last task requires knowledge and skill, as the often-tiny seedlings are hard to tell apart. Several basins were exhibited at the 1972 and 1992 Floriades (international exhibitions of flowers and gardening); the entry for the latter was awarded a gold medal. The basins are a

Bog Pimpernel

perfect way to examine extremely unusual plants from very close up in a small area. Kneel down and admire the enchanting beauty of Bog Pimpernel, the carnivorous Round-leaved Sundew and the Fragrant Orchid. A photographer's macro lens reveals even more of the delicacy of these modest little plants.

Before leaving the nursery, take a look at the herb garden and edible plants on your right as you face the entrance to the nursery: dozens of varieties and strains that humans used in the past or still use today can be found here, including spelt, a primitive variety of hardy wheat that was cultivated by humans as long ago as 7000 BC. It grows between other types of grains that over time were replaced by more productive varieties. Vegetable dye was obtained from Woad, it's yellow flowers producing a blue colour. More well known is the Madder plant, its yellow flowers yielding red dye. A variety of quite rare herbs are grown at the nursery for their seeds, which are later sown in the heemparks and verges in Amstelveen. Harvesting the seeds is simplified by planting in rows: Poppies, Cornflower, Cowherb and Weasel's Snout, Forking Larkspur and Downy Hemp-nettle – all these can be seen here, and all of them once grew in wheat fields. The use of weeding machines, artificial fertilizers, and chemical pesticides, herbicides and fungicides has virtually eliminated them. Quite a few of the hundreds of varieties of indigenous plants that grow in Amstelveen's heemparks are extremely rare; some are even extinct in the wild. The breeding programme at the nursery preserves the original DNA. All in all, the nursery is a wonderful place for horticulturalists, gardeners or landscape architects to acquire knowledge.

We leave the nursery and turn left to continue along the Kwekerijpad. During the summer you stroll through a sea of Devil's-bit Scabious, a lovely representative of the Honeysuckle family. For centuries it has been considered a 'banishing herb', supposedly because it provided protection from witchcraft. On the right of the path, it is combined with Creeping Jenny and violet-coloured Selfheal, a labiate plant that because of its

Growing seeds

19

Constructing and maintaining parks relies heavily on the use of suitable tools; this applies especially to heemparks. Regular visitors to our parks will undoubtedly have seen our staff working with what appear to be outmoded tools. But through the years, experience has shown that the tools that were used to construct the park are still the best. Tens of thousands of cubic metres of mud and peat were removed with dredging nets attached to long poles. They are still used to scrape mud from the bottom of the lake, the water drains through the net, and the sludge is thrown into a boat. The boats are emptied on the shore with a deep shovel. These wooden shovels are more concave than a regular shovel and were specially designed for this work centuries ago. The smaller watercourses are still dredged each year, and the water level in the Dr. Koos Landwehrpark is also maintained with a boat, dredging nets and deep shovels. We still use scythes for much of the mowing, especially in small blossomy meadows and areas where perennials grow, because a brush cutter is less precise and can damage the plants. The reed lands in De Braak were mown with a scythe in years gone by; now it is done with a single-axle lawnmower and a brush cutter. Some parts of the banks are still maintained with a ditch blade and a ditch rake. A ditch blade is a long blade on a pole that resembles a mediaeval halberd. The ditch rake has widely spaced, curved prongs attached to a very long pole. Earlier, a two-handed saw was used to cut logs to insert as reinforcements around the banks; nowadays this is done with a chainsaw, but insofar as it is possible, we prefer to prune by hand. A chainsaw can result in too much material being removed. If a branch of ten centimetres is pruned by hand then you have to be more careful; moreover the result is usually much tidier. Weeding knives – pocketknives with wide blades – have always been the most widely used tool in our parks.

Constructing De Braak, 1941

The Lange Brug leading to Het Eiland

dense inflorescence is also called a 'beehive'. At the end of the small bridge at the right, White Sneezewort is a lovely counterpoint to Brown Knapweed; its powdered leaves are used as sneezing powder, hence it's English name.

Your location now provides you with a broad perspective of the lake and the long bridge at the right that leads to Het Eiland ('The Island'). Broerse had to design his park around the old peat lake, a challenge he took on with relish. According to Broerse, 'If a place has its own atmosphere, the task is to reinforce that', which is why he selected characteristic peat-loving plants for the banks. But first he had to relocate several of the floating islands of reed by cutting them loose with a scythe, dragging them to their new location and securing them with long pointed poles. These poles still exist: just a few years ago while renovating a section of the bank revetments, staff used a winch to extract what they thought was a short pole. It seemed to be endless. The three-and-a-half metre foundation pole with a forty-centimetre wide, pointed base was completely intact.

The parks contain a variety of watercourses and lakes that are all interconnected. The banks are reinforced and protected to prevent them from crumbling away. Reed is used to do this in many places in De Braak. The roots and dead plant material fortify the reedy border against surging waves. If necessary we trim excessively long roots. If a hole appears because of choppy water it is filled in with bits of logs and sometimes Greater Tussock Sedge. Some of the little ditches are more like narrow watercourses, and in these places the natural growth is often dense enough to secure the ground – tree roots are very good for this. We use logs to protect the other banks. These were placed by hand until about 2002, thereafter mechanically when possible. When placing poles by hand the old, usually half-rotten logs were used as foundations for the new ones. Measurements were taken and logs were sawed until they were the correct length – maintaining the height of a shoreline is demanding, precise work. Two men placed logs weighing more than 200 kilograms by hand – if the incorrect length, they were hauled from the water, placed on solid ground and reworked, or the ground beneath them was elevated. This work was done during winter, so labourers stood in their waders in holes in the ice placing logs. Because of Health and Safety laws and common sense, nowadays only the banks that cannot be accessed with a crane are renovated by hand. Precision work of this type is difficult with a crane, so a wall of poles is pushed into the peat to serve as the foundation for the retaining logs. A piece of canvas is stretched along the back of the poles to prevent bank erosion. Logs do not last forever, so they have to be replaced every ten or 20 years, depending on the type of wood (Oak and Elm last a lot longer than Willow or Poplar) and the diameter of the log. Much thicker logs were used in the past, some of them 80 centimetres in diameter.

Relocating the floating islands of reeds gave the large lake in De Braak its current shape. To achieve the correct depth, 10,000 cubic metres of mud was dredged using wooden boats, dredging nets, deep shovels, and sheer hard work. This took a long time, but this was not an issue since the parks were constructed as part of relief work projects. The long bridge would make it possible to walk around the lake. The length of the bridge – too long to harmonise with the surroundings – was broken up by creating a tiny artificial island of reeds just after the halfway point, once again by dragging and securing clumps of reed.

The long bridge ends on **Het Eiland**, which is separated from the land on the east by a narrow ditch. In early spring this area is a riot of purplish-pink Hollowroot, a stinsplant. Its name refers to its hollow roots. The seeds are covered with a sweet substance, relished by ants, which collect the seeds and eat it on their way back to the colony, thereby taking care of the seeds' distribution. Vital to the view are the purple flowers of Hedge Woundwort and Berry Catchfly – rarely found in the wild in the Netherlands, and then only near rivers – and the

Hollowroot

View over Het Eiland

Enchanter's Nightshade that merits a really close look to see the gossamer-thin stamens poking above the calyx. An old superstition said that anyone encountering Enchanter's Nightshade in the forest would lose his or her way.

You leave Het Eiland via the **Drijvend Pad** ('Floating Path'), so named because the ground beneath it was originally too weak to support it. Many bundles of branches and stalks were laid crosswise on the path, and rubble and other robust materials were placed on top to create a solid foundation. Osiers sprout from low stems between the reeds lining both sides of the path. Continuing further we see the same tree in its more familiar truncated form. These willow trees were included by

Purple Toothwort

Broerse to show the interrelations between nature and culture. In years gone by, especially willows were planted to provide wood for future use. Pollard willows were sawn off at a certain height, after which they re-sprouted around the cut. Wicker baskets, hoops and mats were made from the osiers. Larger pieces of wood were used for tools or firewood. As a pollard

Osier beds and pollard willows

For centuries, if not thousands of years, people have made good use of the rapid growth rate and elasticity of willows. They have other advantages too: they grow in places where very few 'useful' plants survive – wet, soggy places, even swamps that flood at high tide – and you only have to poke a willow branch into the ground and it roots. Yet another advantage is that if a willow is sawn down, it regrows beautiful long, straight branches.

Already in the Iron Age osiers were used to weave panels from which houses were constructed. Pollard willows have grown in the Netherlands for over 2000 years. There are two types of pollard willows, and both of these grow in the park. The 'ordinary' pollard willow is usually trimmed to between one-and-a-half and two-metres in height, which produces its crown. These willows guaranteed the farmer's future wood stock and thus were not grown commercially. Osier beds are fields with wet ground where willows are planted in rows. These trees are sawn off

between 20 and 50 centimetres above the ground. In effect, these osier beds are 'willow plantations' that are pruned yearly. They produce long, thin, pliable branches that are used to make baskets, hoops, nesting boxes for ducks, snares, hoop nets and suchlike. Depending on their thickness, the branches can be used for handles for tools, beanpoles, stakes, firewood and also fascine mattresses – mats of woven willow that, when weighed down with stones, are sunk into water to become part of the foundations for a new dyke. The Netherlands owes a great deal to these trees. While designing the three heemparks, Chris Broerse doubtless recalled the pollard willows that grew throughout Zeeland where he grew up. It is because of these memories that the different varieties of willow are so prevalent in the parks. Due to the unfortunate declining demand for wicker, many osier beds have been removed, although some can still be found in South Holland, Utrecht and Brabant.

willow ages, hollows appear in the trunk that serve as nesting places for ducks, little owls and other birds. Bats also like these hollows. Pollard willows have to be constantly pruned otherwise they eventually topple under their own weight.

Purple Toothwort grows beneath willows during spring. This is a parasite that draws nourishment from the roots of willows and other trees, which appear to be unaffected by its presence. The only parts of the plant that are visible are the large, flat salvia-like flowers.

This path ends in the **Elsrijklaan**, the former driveway leading to Elsrijk manor, less than 100 metres from the Banpaal, in popular parlance 'de Naald' ('the Needle'), on the Amsterdamseweg. This banishing pole is best seen from the pavement outside, so leave the park for a moment, turn right and take 20 paces. The history of this location can be traced to 1565 when there was a residence here for the children of Mayor Hillebrantszoon of Amsterdam. Later inhabitants named the homestead 'Braeckrijk', after the little lake De Braak that was formed by a collapse in the peat dyke. The Elskamp family, who lived here towards the end of the seventeenth century, wanted

The Elsrijk manor, with left the banishing pole and tea cupola at right. Engraving from 1737

The banishing pole

Banishing poles are stone obelisks that were placed around a city to mark its borders, and beyond which a person banished from the city could not pass. This pole dates from 1625, when justice was administered on a very local level and being banned from a city (or anywhere) was a widespread punitive measure. It is placed at a distance of 1000 rods ('roedes') from the city centre. An Amsterdam rod was equivalent to roughly 3.68 metres. This banishing pole therefore indicated a distance of nearly 3,7 kilometres. This sandstone pillar rests on a brick plinth. Closer inspection of the seams between the bricks might reveal Spleenwort.

The text on the pole reads: *'Terminus, Proscriptions, uijtterste palen der Ballingen'*. The Dutch text is a free translation of the Latin that precedes it, meaning 'uttermost banishing pole'. The stonecutter was in all likelihood a poorly educated man: he forgot the 'o' in the word 'pro', which can be seen outside the small plaque. The law of excommunication was enforced until 1795. The banishing pole is on ground that is still within Amsterdam city limits.

their name – and that of the many Alders ('Els' in Dutch) that stood here – to be connected to the location, so they renamed it Elsrijk ('Alder Kingdom'). It developed into a prosperous homestead that saw the addition – several generations later – of a real Chinese tent on a former tea cupola in the lake. Along with large numbers of exotic water birds the scene must have been especially appealing. Yet, it is not only nature that passes: the buildings were demolished in 1796, leaving only the gateway. This has long since disappeared too. Looking at this view while standing beside the banishing pole, there is nothing that remains of the homestead... until you see a duck that looks like it is standing on the surface of the water. It is actually perched on one of the Chinese tent's foundation poles.

Because of the settled ground beneath the old driveway, the area to the right of the path is the only place in De Braak where old and large trees grow. The ground elsewhere is too soggy and trees struggle to root and achieve full stature. This lane is

View across the large lake from the Elsrijklaan. The Salvation Army Training College in the background was demolished in 2003.

beautiful in spring, when the Primrose here flowers light yellow. Further along patches of Cowberry cover the ground. Also resplendent is the Rough Horsetail that thrives here in giant form. The stiff stems are reminiscent of bamboo and cast mesmerising shadows when the sun shines through them.

When you get to the intersection of four paths, stay on the Elsrijklaan by walking down the second path from the left ahead of you. In spring the ground is covered with Wood Anemones. Many people are unaware that this beautiful, fragile plant is poisonous; the sap can irritate the skin. The flowers are heliotropic, meaning they follow the sun. Slightly later in the season the small white star-shaped flowers of Wild Garlic nod hypnotically in the breeze, and the oniony odour this herb emanates is difficult to avoid in this area. The leaves are delicious in soup, in herb butter or with cheese in a sandwich. Herb Paris with its rigid garlands of four, sometimes five oval leaves waves jauntily in the breeze. During the summer its tempting yet poisonous blue-black berries protrude five centimetres above the leaves.

On both sides of the path you will notice several multi-stemmed Black Alders. These were planted before the Second World War as a single tree, but fuel shortages during the last years of the Occupation resulted in it being sawn off close to

Herb Paris

Cross-leaved Heath

the ground, causing it to produce multiple stems. They characterise this path and have inspired park keepers to introduce the idea of multi-stemmed trees elsewhere in Amstelveen. The almost transparent looking Wood Horsetail lends the atmosphere of a watercolour to this scene, the colours gently flowing from light to dark.

At the next intersection the Elsrijklaan changes into **De Doorbraak**. Keep going straight ahead and you will see the second lake in the park that was added in 1941 because the previous relief work projects employing navvies and farmhands from the borough were not yet sufficiently mitigated. Almost four hectares would be added to De Braak, requiring 600 man-weeks of work. The lake had to be excavated, paths laid and dams and culverts built where the paths crossed the water. Because this was not a natural lake, Broerse was free to design the surroundings as he saw fit, and surprisingly, this time he opted for cultivated plants, and not wild plants, as long as they were indigenous to the Netherlands. Based on the groundwater level the planting was done in layers. Alders with a ground cover of Broad Buckler Fern grow in the lower areas, and higher areas are home to Bog Myrtle, Creeping Willow and Cross-leaved Heath, interspersed with the pinkish tints of Crown Vetch and the

De Doorbraak, seen from the start of the Taxodiumpad

Constructing De Doorbraak, 1941

brighter Maiden Pink. Cross-leaved Heath predominates here, but looking closely you will see Heather with its squamous leaves; this is a foreign natural hybrid, a cross between Cross-leaved Heath and the foreign *Erica x watsonii*. Broerse named this section of the park 'De Doorbraak' ('The Transition'), because people 'leaving nature (wild flora) arrive in culture (exotics), or, in reverse, going from culture people end up in nature ...'.

When you arrive at the fork at the end of this path, sit for a moment on one of the two benches at the beginning of the **Taxodiumpad** on the left, which offer a view lengthways over the lake. At left is the majestic Weeping Willow you passed earlier, its branches drooping just above the water; further away are the two dark green pine trees, flanked by groups of Taxodiums (flood-tolerant conifers) that give this path its name. Human interventions are clearly visible in the truncated branches. Their peculiar shapes certainly

Shallon, with Sarcococca in the foreground

contribute to an unusual view that according to some has a touch of the antediluvian. Taxodiums originated in the southern swamps of North America and can become extremely old, growing to more than 40 metres tall. In spring, this side of the lake is a pinkish-red sea of exotic Rhododendrons and Azaleas. Compare this view to a black-and-white photograph from 1941 showing the construction of this section of the park. A bare polder landscape has been transformed into an idyllic sanctuary, testifying to the vision, effort and dedication of the labourers working only with spades and wheelbarrows. Beside and in front of the bench that you're sitting on you see Sarcococca. When it flowers in winter and early spring, it releases a lovely lemony scent. Just behind the benches is a ginkgo. It is the only survivor of a distinct order of gymnosperms that saw their heyday 65 million years ago; in effect, this is a living fossil.

Continuing along the path, on the right you see several gnarled dead trunks of an old Yew tree or Taxus, in this instance the cultivar *Taxus baccata* 'Dovastonii'. All species of Taxus are poisonous. In the Netherlands it only grows wild around Winterswijk in the east of the country. It produces strong, pliable wood, which resulted in it being used for bows and tool handles during the Stone Age. In front of the Yew trees are groups of short Swiss Willows, and in summer Heather blooms here. An occasional Rampion Bellflower raises its head above the muddle. Since the Middle Ages this Campanula has been consumed as a raw vegetable – it's roots have a soft radish-like flavour. At left is a large Horse Chestnut, a variety brought from South-East Europe and Turkey. Its fruit is inedible and was formerly used as medicine for livestock: it could help cure a horse's cough, hence its name. The creeper *Gaultheria shallon* or Shallon, the leaves of which are frequently used in bouquets, grows to the left of the path.

Yew

Wood Stichwort

The Taxodiumpad veers to the right, becoming the **Prinsessen-laantje**, which is planted on both sides with Greater Celandine, bright white-blossoming Wood Stitchwort, and yellowish-white Pale Corydalis. Very inconspicuous yet prevalent everywhere is the Broad-leaved Helleborine, a wild member of the orchid family with a somewhat opaque russet colour. As usual, we advise you to get up close to see these flowers in detail.

The Prinsessenlaantje leads you out of the park, but it's too early for that, so return to the Taxodiumpad and keep walking until you reach the junction with De Doorbraak on the right. Turn left over a watercourse that well nigh criss-crosses the entire park and then take an immediate right turn onto the **Bospad**. Dog's Mercury with rather nondescript white flowers lines the edges of the path. It releases an unpleasant odour if damaged or bruised – a good thing too, because it is poisonous for man and beast alike. Wild Daffodil and Yellow Anemone are first to bloom in spring, followed a little later by Yellow Archangel.

The path takes its name, which translates as 'Forest Path', from the Birch, Alder, Alder Buckthorn, Common Beech and Hawthorn that grow here. The Hazel trees have been here since the park was constructed. The ground is covered with Polypody.

The **Boshyacintenpad** is the first path on the right. Suppose you had eaten some poisonous Dog's Mercury... well, here you could pick Common Vincetoxicum, highly toxic too, but also an emetic, which is why it has

Broad-leaved Helleborine

English Bluebell

The Van Leerpad

been used for centuries as an antidote. Whether it actually helps
is questionable though, and it is wisest not to pick any plants.
The English Bluebell, with its sweet-scented purple flowers, covers
the ground like a carpet in spring. Pause for a moment on the
little bridge at the end of the path and admire the lovely tranquil
view along the banks of the watercourse lined with ferns, with the
sunlight breaking through the foliage and dancing on the water.

Return again to the Bospad, which becomes the **Van Leerpad**.
An open patch of land on both sides of the path offers a
panoramic view, on the right of De Doorbraak, and on the left
of the stylish architecture of the Van Leer company that used to
have a packaging factory on the opposite side. Broerse also
designed the terrain around the company buildings as a heempark that the municipality maintained. The path you are on
now was part of the industrial terrain and was later purchased

The Van Leerpad with a view over the pool

from the company for a symbolic amount. Broerse designed the parks such that – when looking out from his house – he had an unrestricted view across De Doorbraak and this part of the path in the Van Leerpark.

This is an area that is beautiful regardless of the season, with powerfully coiled fern fronds in spring; serenity and subtle shades of green during summer; contrasts between the yellowing leaves on the trees, the fern fronds and the green mosses in autumn; with the frost in winter adding yet more sharpness to the variations in structure. The very rare Common Wintergreen – a short perennial with incredibly fine seeds (250,000 seeds weigh a gram) – can be found between the Bog Myrtle shrubs. Numerous water plants grow by the lake such as the stately Flowering Rush, the unremarkable Marsh Arrowgrass, and the white-blossomed Bogbean. It is a pity they are too far away to admire in detail, especially as the petals of the Buckbean flowers are covered with fine white hairs.

Unfortunately, after the Van Leer park closed in the 1970s, the heem tradition on the Van Leer terrain was neglected. On

Bogbean

Taxodiums at De Doorbraak, seen from the Van Leerpad

Moss Rockbrake

the park side, however, the combination of Bog Rosemary with the yellow of Creeping Willow is a feast for the eyes. Cranberry plants, their fruit served with game, cover the landscape with a thick woolly carpet, supplemented further ahead on the right by the soft hills of Moss Rockbrake leading to the water – beautiful to look at but a invasive disaster if left alone too long. Here and there between the heather grows Mountain Tobacco or Wolf's Bane, better known as (Mountain) Arnica and widely used medicinally because of its healing properties. Mountain tobacco used to be added to snuff, because the dried leaves irritate the mucous membranes in the nostrils.

Leaving the open area, you arrive at another intersection of four paths. Take a peek at the **Christoffelpad** on the right, named after the Herb Christopher, commonly called Baneberry, and the Wood Sorrel that line the path. Honeysuckle twines up the trees.

Then head left at the intersection and continue straight ahead along **De Steiger**, a cul-de-sac that has a lovely view of the Van Leer terrain and the water in front of it. A bench invites you to sit down, and while you pause for a breather, take a good look at the yolk-yellow flowers of the Common Fleabane growing nearby. This plant was used to treat dysentery. On your walk back

Common Fleabane

Scotch Mist

Angled Solomon's Seal

you will not fail to notice the Scotch Mist that grows here along with Wood Melick. Scotch Mist has been extinct in the wild in the Netherlands since 1978.

Bear left off De Steiger and proceed along the second part of the **Van Leerpad**. You have probably already seen it in the park, but here it is especially conspicuous: Solomon's Seal, recognisable from its drooping stalks with long rows of white, pendent, bell-shaped flowers. Each year the old stalk breaks off the rootstock and the fracture somewhat resembles an official seal, hence the 'Seal' in its common name. Saw-wort, its name an obvious reference to its serrated leaves, has not been seen in the wild in the Netherlands since 1977. A fine yellow dye is extracted from leaves of this purple-flowering plant. Also prevalent are Heather, Common Juniper, Proliferous Pink and, in spring, especially Wild Tulip. It is the only variety of tulip that grows in the wild in the Netherlands, and was first described in 1568. This yellow-flowering stinsplant is usually planted on homesteads.

The Hoge Brug

The Van Leerpad connects with the Elsrijklaan, where you turn
right towards the **Hoge Brug**, the area leading to it
characterised by thick clumps of Greater Tussock Sedge. To the
right of the bridge is a view of the fenced Hein Koningenbos,
named after the man who, as chief inspector at Amstelveen's
Parks and Public Gardens Department between 1975 and 2001,
was a tireless proponent of the heemparks. Much of the time
the park keepers still use the old name for this restricted
terrain, Vogelbos ('Bird Forest'). The front part of the grove is
used to decompose plant waste into various types of compost.

The Hoge Brug continues as the **Spirealaantje**, named after the tall, creamy-white flowering *Spirea*, colloquially Meadowsweet (Queen of the Meadows), that walls both sides of the path. This plant was used to treat biliousness, kidney ailments, gout and neuralgia. The buds contain aspirin-like compounds that have remedial properties. The abundance of Purple Loosestrife completes this view. This pathway ends at the Amsterdamse-weg, which you can cross to get to the entrance to the Dr. Koos Landwehrpark.

The Dr. Koos Landwehrpark

You are entering a park that is a dramatic contrast to De Braak in size and atmosphere. It measures but half a hectare and was constructed on a wet, nutrient-poor patch of meadow. You make your way via a winding path to slightly lower ground, where you will undoubtedly notice the Holly that has truly stretched its branches. Common Holly is one of the plants that symbolise Christmas. The prickly leaves and red fruits actually represent the Crucifixion, so it may seem unusual that Holly is associated with the birth of Christ, but this is because the fruits disappear around Easter time. Before Europe was Christianised, Holly – because it is an evergreen – represented eternity and hope for the spring. Follow this path and turn left at the intersection. If you look in the direction of the Amsterdamseweg, you will see a border with Burnet Rose, a beautiful wild variety that was among the first flowers to be cultivated by humans.

Blossomy grasslands

Southern Marsh-orchid

Here too, Broerse used the natural environment as the basis to create a soggy, flowery infertile meadow on the marshy, nutrient-poor peat. Yellow Rattle blooms alongside the path; the roots of this semi-parasite seek out the roots of other plants such as grass or clover from which it derives its nourishment. Its impact on its surroundings is evident in the shorter length of the grass around it. But other plants benefit from this: the Broad-leaved Helleborine and the Western Marsh Orchid. Fritillary grows well here too; in June its delicate tulip-like purple and white chequered flowers peer through the grass.

Looking to the right of the path across the meadow, you will see three different grass 'environments'. The area where you are standing is rich in nutrients. Across the water is a strip of half nutrient rich land that runs all the way to the small playground on the right, and behind this and immediately

Dr. Koos Landwehr (1911–96)

Jacobus ('Koos') Landwehr was born the son of a textile merchant in Kampen in 1911. At the age of five he moved to Amstelveen. He gained a landscaping diploma and later a degree as a lecturer in horticulture. He ran a flower nursery with his brother until 1938. When they and their nursery were evicted to make way for part of the Amsterdamse Bos, he started working for Amstelveen municipality. He was soon noticed for his knowledge of Dutch flora, and Broerse made good use of his knowhow when constructing the heemparks. Landwehr travelled throughout the Netherlands in search of plants and much of the credit for obtaining the indigenous plants that grow in Amstelveen's heemparks must go to him. His experience as a nurseryman led to him running the heemplant nursery in De Braak. For years he was second in charge at the municipality's Parks & Public Gardens Department, responsible for work in the field. He developed the stewardship of the heemparks that has remained largely unchanged to this day.

Like most 'heem lovers' of his generation, he was a man of knowledge, but was very forthright and stern with his staff. He could usually be found outside, in the park, among the plants. Still doing the rounds are tales of how he corrected mistakes or carelessness by his staff by throwing a stone or a clod of dirt to indicate an area that had to be raised or lowered. He also used to brazenly pull out plants if these were not placed to his liking.

Dr. Koos Landwehrpark after mowing

He shared his botanical knowledge by making drawings of and writing about Dutch and European flora. He produced several compendiums about Dutch grasses, mosses and liverworts. His masterpiece – still cherished far and wide – is undoubtedly the two-volume *Wilde Orchideeën van Europa* ('Wild Orchids of Europe'), published in 1977 by Natuurmo-numenten. He and Cees Sipkes published the book *Wilde planten-tuinen* ('Wild Gardens') in 1974. He illustrated all these books with amazing pen and ink drawings and watercolours. In 1972 Landwehr received the Heimans and Thijsse Prize for his field biology research. The University of Amsterdam awarded him an honorary degree in 1985, acknowledging his services to botany.

Koos Landwehr retired in 1975 and moved to France where he continued writing and drawing. After his sudden death in 1996 a number of friends and colleagues began an initiative to have the Mauritsplantsoen, a small heempark near De Braak and the Dr. Jac. P. Thijssepark, renamed Dr. Koos Landwehrpark in his honour. This did occur in 1997. As a further commemoration a basalt pillar with a small plaque was placed by the entrance to the park. The text on it translates as:

Dr. J. Landwehr, 1911-1996,
A Grand Master of horticulture.
Honorary Doctor at the University of Amsterdam.
Re-created flora in the Netherlands in Amstelveen's heemparks.
A gifted illustrator of grasses, mosses and orchids.

opposite is an area that is clearly darker with a bluish-green tint: the so-called Molinia meadow that has the least nutrients. Varieties that grow here include Meadow Thistle, Lesser Spearwort, Devil's-bit Scabious, Marsh Lousewort and Whorled Caraway, the latter now extinct in the Netherlands. The differences in nutrient values are carefully maintained by mowing the meadow twice annually and removing the raked up cuttings. This corresponds to the earlier practise of mowing areas like this and saving the hay as fodder for sheep during winter. Animals are sometimes set to graze on the heath in summer. The manure is mixed with sods of peat and strewn on the arable land to render it suitable for farming. The meadows were used exclusively for growing hay, with a consequent reduction in nutrients. This means that only plants that can thrive in nutrient-poor soil had a chance. In a nutrient-rich meadow they would immediately be replaced by varieties such as Meadow Buttercup, Common Sorrel and Common Dandelion. After artificial fertilisers were introduced, people fertilised meadows elsewhere in the Netherlands to increase yields. This resulted in Molinia meadows becoming more rare and now the Dr. Koos Landwehrpark is one of the few places

Devil's-bit Scabious

Fenland with Water Soldier and Yellow Rattle in the foreground

Water Soldier

where we can still see varieties of plants that 'belong' in this characteristic grassland.

The path you are on crosses the park diagonally, bringing you closer to the water, where the tips of Water Soldier emerge from the water in summer. Its white flowers protrude above the surface in May to June, and when the water cools down during autumn, the plant sinks to the bottom to hibernate. In spring it resurfaces with new, bright green leaves. This plant has an important role in creating land in fenlands.

Regal Ferns surrounded by Fritillary

Turn right at the crossroads and you immediately encounter Regal Ferns on both sides of the path. This is a truly majestic plant that under ideal conditions – such as those they enjoy here – can grow to between two and three metres in height and live for 100 years. In winter and spring you can clearly see how old these plants are, their gnarled bases resembling Chinese mountain landscapes. During summer the left of the path is also home to Cabbage Thistle, at a metre-and-a-half tall a worthy neighbour to the Regal Ferns.

Turn right at the streetlamp onto the asphalt street in front of you, the Mauritslaan. The border on your right hand side is planted with Burnet Rose. It blooms from May to June with glorious creamy-white flowers that later change into unusual black rosehips. From here you can look across the roses towards the Molinia meadow again, with Meadow Thistle, a plant that thrives in these soil conditions that blooms crimson in summer. Further along, a sloping path to the right takes you back down into the park itself. There is a hedgerow on your left that originated as Field Maple. This slow-growing tree – they can live for 300 years – is usually pruned to make hedgerows, and the branches are used to make small tools or handles. The bark doesn't shed after it has been felled, making it highly suitable wood for chicken perches – the fowls' feet don't freeze and they keep a firm grip because of the texture of the bark. The foliage was used for fodder and maple trees also make good firewood. Over the years other varieties sprouted amid the hedgerow and these are pruned along with it: Holly, Elderberry and Red Dogwood are common. In general, the more varieties, the older the hedgerow.

Behind the low wooden fence on your right is part of the half nutrient rich grassland, home to Sweet Vernal Grass, also called vanilla grass for its distinctive fragrance in summer. The dried stalks were used as flavouring for drinks and punches. The vanilla scent, coumarin, also occurs in Sweet Woodruff, and is used to flavour May wine. Butterflies love grasslands; here you will encounter the Meadow Brown and the Six-spot Burnet, actually a daytime moth, nicknamed Blood Drop Burnett Moth or Blood Droplet Moth after the red patches on its glossy black wings.

The best way to leave the Dr. Koos Landwehrpark is by returning to the Mauritslaan and then turning left past the Burnet Roses onto the Emmakade that follows the Hoornsloot. If you continue bearing left, you will see the entrance to the Dr. Jac. P. Thijssepark on the Prins Bernhardlaan.

The Dr. Jac. P. Thijssepark

Construction on this park started two years after De Braak, in
1941, driven by the same need to provide relief work. It was
part of the development plan totalling 24 hectares that was
anticipated on the Westelijke Bovenlanden ('Western
Meadows') of the Buitenveldertse polder. The Hoornsloot, the
Landscheidingsvaart and the Oude Karselaan separated this
piece of land from the Amsterdamse Bos, which would serve as

The Orchideeënstuk

a transition between the woods and the residences that would be built here. The sale of expensive houses came to a virtual standstill with the outbreak of World War Two, and the decision was made to accelerate the parks' construction to attract potential house buyers.

Originally this area was a low-lying, soggy meadow with poor soil quality. The average height of the ground itself was 1.39 metres below Normal Amsterdam Water Level (NAP), with the groundwater level at 1.55 metres below NAP: obviously an

Jac. P. Thijsse

Jacobus Pieter Thijsse (1865–1945) was a teacher, field biologist and conservationist who avidly promoted nature in the Netherlands. He is especially remembered for his Verkade albums, in which purchasers could affix stickers with images of nature that came with Verkade products (mainly biscuits). Thijsse made nineteen of these from 1906; the first issues were titled *Lente, Zomer, Herfst* and *Winter* ('Spring', 'Summer', 'Autumn', 'Winter'). Earlier he and his friend Eli Heimans wrote the series of children's books *Van vlinders, bloemen en vogels* ('About Butterflies, Flowers and Birds'), in which they encouraged youngsters to explore nature for themselves. In 1896 Thiisse and Heimans started the journal *De Levende Natuur* ('Living Nature') with J. Jaspers Jr.; it is still published today, albeit with substantial changes to the content. The book *Heimans, Heinsius en Thijsse's geïllustreerde flora van Nederland* ('Heimans, Heinsius and Thijsse's Illustrated Flora of the Netherlands') appeared in 1899 and unlike similar books this one had illustrations and familiar names. The authors drew the 3400 illustrations in the book themselves. It was a perfect beginner's guide.

Thijsse was also a driving force behind the formation of the Vereniging tot Behoud van Natuurmonumenten in Nederland (Society for the Preservation of Nature Reserves in the Netherlands). The then-municipal University of Amsterdam awarded him an honorary doctorate on 16 October 1922.

Thijsse was a great advocate of including wild, indigenous plants in so-called educational public gardens and parks, such as Thijsse's Hof in Bloemendaal, constructed in 1925. Still open today, plants and animals from Zuid-Kennermerland are displayed to a broad public among natural habitats that include dune forests, thickets, dune grasslands and dune valley vegetation. The phrase 'educational public gardens and parks' was replaced later by 'heemparks'. Indisputably, Jac. P. Thijsse's approach formed the basis for Chris Broerse's ideas. The Westelijk Bovenpark was re-baptised the Dr. Jac. P. Thijssepark in 1953.

Jac. P. Thijsse

The hill with Dark Mullein and Crown Vetch

impossible situation when considering that to grow properly, trees require at least one-and-a-half metres between ground level and groundwater. Broerse decided to excavate a number of deep lakes and use the removed peat to elevate other sections of the park. This would have been enough, were it not for him planning a five-metre tall hill in the far north-west of the park that would look over Amsterdamse Bos. Lacking peat, he asked the municipality to dump 5400 cubic metres of domestic and urban rubbish in the park – at the time the usual way to prepare soggy peat land for construction. The foundations of several streets in this neighbourhood were created this way too, as was part of the moist meadowland around the Poel. Ground like this was known colloquially as 'asland' ('ashland'). Some of the rubbish – ash from fires, old shoes, earthenware shards and old metal – did not decay, or only did so very slowly, making it ideal material, because it subsided only slightly in comparison to peat. The man-hours required to accomplish this plan were estimated at 2300.

After raising the hill, the work came to a standstill in 1942 because the Germans were sending growing numbers of unemployed Dutch nationals to work in Germany. The nitrogen-rich hill was soon festooned with stinging nettles, but that did have its benefits. Koos Landwehr, who was also involved in structuring the Thijssepark, was a member of the resistance. When, every now and again, the Germans got too close for comfort, he rowed a boat from his nearby house in the Oud-Patrimonium neighbourhood, via the Landscheidings-vaart, to the hiding place he had excavated in the hill of rubbish. The stinging nettles obscured the entrance and kept the curious at bay.

Yellow Archangel

Pasqueflower

Pasqueflower, going to seed

The story of how and when the rest of the park came about will unfold before you once you start your stroll on the **Heidepad**. The roof of foliage above you is formed by 70-year-old trees, some wrapped in winding Hop tendrils. In spring Yellow Archangel flowers along the paths, along with Wood Stitchwort with its pretty fragile white flowers, and the purple Hollowroot, a stinsplant. The beautiful purple flowers of Pasqueflower appear in March; this is an unusual plant because – apart from its flowers – it is covered with fluffy 'hair' from top to bottom, making it resemble a 'wild man'. It is said that anyone eating this toxic plant will laugh so much they will die from it.

The Bog Myrtle flanking the path is particularly impressive when the crowns of the trees part and the sun illuminates the first so-called garden room. This beautiful robust shrub appears in April and can grow to a height of two metres. Rub a leaf between your fingers to release the ethereal oils that have resulted in this plant's remarkable history. The scientific name is *Myrica gale;* 'gale' is an old Celtic word for balsam. The resin has been used for centuries to treat skin diseases and toothache, among others. Bog Myrtle has also been used for centuries as a flea and

The Heidepad with a view of Bog Myrtle and Common Foxglove, Creeping Willow in the foreground

mosquito repellent. Although the plant is slightly toxic, the leaves were and are used in Germany to flavour stews (like Bay leaves) and sometimes to preserve beer. Bog Myrtle is one of the naturally occurring plants in the Netherlands most

targeted by thieves. The branches with their pretty catkins are very popular in flower arrangements. Park employees have sometimes stood guard for nights at a time when professional Bog Myrtle traders from Brabant came to steal our plants.

The Doctrine of Signatures

Literature on medicinal plants widely cites the Doctrine of Signatures, a classical/mediaeval theory that maintains that certain physical attributes of plants serve as signs that indicate their therapeutic value. But before any serious research could be conducted into the healing properties of plants, signs of God had to first be sought in them. Anything could be an indication: colour, shapes of parts of the plant, hairiness, the inflorescence and when it occurred, and so on. In antiquity this was combined with astrology. Colour was the first to be assessed. Yellow was associated with the digestive system, red with the heart and blood, blue with the airways. The shape of the leaves was also a determining factor: heart-shaped leaves were good for the heart, kidney-shaped leaves for the kidneys, and so forth. Other external characteristics such as hairiness (mucous membranes) or hollow stems (gullet and bronchi) were also important. People identified the small oil glands in the leaves of Perforate St John's Wort with pores in human skin, so the plant was thought to help with skin diseases. Most of these attributes have meanwhile been proven wrong, yet some plants do have properties that can be associated with their external characteristics. Walnuts, which resemble brains, contain fats that actually are good for the brain, and Lungwort, with its long, hairy leaves, which also have white 'alveoli', contain saponins that do work as a mild expectorant. Whether these are signs from God or pure coincidence is not for us to decide.

Lungwort

Water Avens

Once you reach the end of the path – still under the leafy roof –
you will see an ocean of Water Avens on both sides. This somewhat hairy plant has beautiful russet-coloured, nodding flowers.
Its name is derived from its burr-like seeds with hooked or jointed
tips that are distributed by being caught in the coats of animals.

The Heidepad splits into the Klimoppad on the left and the
Bosbespad on the right. Start by taking 30 paces along the
Klimoppad and having a look at the fine view of the second
garden room in the Thijssepark, which is transversed by the
Bosbespad, and which we will get to in a while. From here it is
easy to see how the Thijssepark differs from De Braak in every
way. In De Braak Broerse wanted to emphasise the scenic
beauty and capture the interplay between water, heathland,
woods and reeds in panoramic views. However, he decided to

View through to the Amsterdamse Bos with Meadow Crane's-bill in the foreground

deal with the Thijssepark – often no wider than 50 metres – in completely different ways. Here he designed semi-enclosed 'garden rooms', each with their own atmosphere, each a pleasantly surprising place to pause on the winding pathways. By continuously altering structure, colour, openness and intimacy, Broerse succeeded in making a walk through the park a true journey of exploration, with new places and views around every corner. He used the Amsterdamse Bos in the background to maximum effect to create panoramas. From the Klimoppad you can clearly see the bright green 'moustache' of ferns along the waterside, and behind this, the heathland and short blueberry plants that gradually make way for the slightly taller German Greenweed, Purple Chokeberry, and finally the

Hawthorns and Black Alders that serve as the 'walls' of this garden room. A gap in the trees offers another view, this time over the Hoornsloot, of the Amsterdamse Bos, creating enormous depth of field. Ahead of you the path's verge twinkles with the bobbing yellow flowers of the Wild Daffodil or Trumpet Narcissus. This plant is named after the mythical Greek hunter who was so adored by all he met that he asked the gods to allow him to experience unrequited love. Aphrodite consented and made him fall in love with his own reflection, and he pined away and perished. Aphrodite took pity on him and transformed him into this flower. Between June and August, Meadow Crane's-bill flowers purplish-blue here.

Meadow Crane's-bill

Turn round and walk back to the intersection and cross the
little bridge on your left onto the semi-circular **Bosbespad**, the
path you were looking at from your vantage point on the
Klimoppad a few moments ago. From the bridge, you might
see and smell the Honeysuckle blossoms in summer at the left.
The view to the right from the bridge is also worth it: Regal
Ferns and branches drooping low over the water make this an
idyllic scene. To the left of the path, Purple Chokeberry, a
hybrid of red and black chokeberry shrubs imported from
North America in circa 1700. It is regarded as a marsh pest
because birds disseminate its seeds throughout peat lands in

The beginning of the Bosbespad, seen from the bridge

the Netherlands, where it can interfere with the formative stages of a marshland, resulting in large areas being choked by Magellan's Sphagnum. It takes on a beautiful hue in autumn. The berries don't taste that remarkable or special, which means their juice can be used as an almost flavourless additive to other fruit juices. A few steps along on the right, Highbush Blueberry, imported around 1770 from North America and now established in Drenthe, Gelderland and Overijssel, bears sweet and tasty fruit.

The path is lined with prickly German Greenweed that flowers yellow in May and June. Further along in an open section three types of heather grow all in a muddle: in higher,

drier areas the rare Bell Heather (in the Netherlands only found on high sandy ground along the Maas in Limburg); in the wetter areas Cross-leaved Heath; and in the remaining parts, Heather. Teetering on the banks are enormous patches of yellow Marsh St. John's Wort flanked by Bog Asphodel. The bench to the right, beside the Hoornsloot, is a good place to take in your surroundings. Close by, Bittersweet Nightshade, which flowers purplish-blue all summer, can be recognised from its bright yellow, entangled stamens. A relative of Nightshade, it takes its name from its flavour – first bitter, then sweet. Ancient Egyptians bestowed a ritual significance on this plant: Tutankhamen's mummy was found with a string of Bittersweet berries round his neck. Farmers in Germany used to hang strings of these berries round their livestock's necks to protect them from evil. These so-called banishing herbs are also called 'witch herbs'. Orphine, a plant you will encounter just ahead on the right had a similar function.

Marsh St. John's Wort

Orphine

Summer Snowflake

We leave the Bosbespad via another little bridge and begin our stroll along the **Klokjespad**, which provides a view of Het Orchideeën-stuk ('The Orchid Track'), where we will get to shortly; ignore the side paths and bridges leading off this path for now, too. From April to June the Summer Snowflake's characteristic little white bell-shaped flowers bob in the breeze; these are finished with a dainty green dot at the end of each tepal. During summer the red-flowering Rosebay Willowherb can be seen here and there; this is a well-known plant frequently encountered in nitrogen-rich soil, where, for example, there was a fire, or the ground has been churned. Other plants adding colour to this border are Goldilocks Buttercup and Ragged Robin, the latter taking its name from the foam that in days gone by was thought to be cuckoo saliva. It is actually deposited by the Meadow Froghopper, a bug that makes a foam nest of saliva for its larvae on the Ragged Robin, among others.

Deadly Nightshade, flowering and with berries

The Klokjespad ends with a poisonous corridor. Belladonna or Deadly Nightshade grows to a metre-and-a-half in height, and is so toxic that symptoms of poisoning appear after consuming a mere 0,3 grams of it. The generic name 'belladonna' *(Atropa belladonna)* means 'beautiful woman' in Italian. During the Renaissance women used eye drops made from this atropine-containing plant to enlarge their pupils and make them darker and shiny, just like the plant's black berries. The damage to their eyesight was overshadowed by their vanity. Atropine is still used by opthalmists but only in minute quantities. Herb Paris and Baneberry, also called Herb Christopher, are slightly less poisonous. St. Christopher is not only the patron saint of sailors

Herb Christopher, flowering and with berries

and travellers; he also protects those stricken by sudden illness. Small quantities of Herb Christopher were believed to be a remedy for this.

Walk back about 30 metres and stop at the entrance to the pathway leading to Het Orchideeënstuk. Opposite the path is a small Medlar tree, which produces fruit in summer measuring about 3 or 4 centimetres in diameter. This plant is largely remembered because of a famous saying: 'as rotten as a Medlar'. The fruit cannot be eaten fresh – it first has to rot on the ground for a while before a preserve can be made from it that is delicious with game.

View of the Orchideeënstuk

Now cross the little bridge that takes you to **Het Orchideeën-stuk**. The bridge is surrounded by the lush foliage of Maidenhair Spleenwort and Heart's Tongue Fern, with companions Pellitory-of-the-Wall, Yellow Corydalis and Hard Shield Fern. An overarching Black Alder branch above your head frames this idyllic scene (see the title page for a photograph), a view already captured by Koos Landwehr in his drawings and paintings. A vista such as this underscores the necessity of including the passage of time itself when designing, constructing and maintaining a heempark. In De Braak you saw the extent to which an artificial lake and the

plants lining its shore have become a fully-fledged landscape with giant trees and plants in only 50 years. In many ways it looks like it has always been there. The same principle applies here: as wooded areas age they become more valuable, not only in terms of aesthetics and sentimental value, but they take on a greater ecological significance too. Maintenance is equally important in this progression: what can be pruned to make room for other plants and how will it be pruned? Some trees are pruned so that they have a gnarled trunk and grow low horizontal branches: purely for how they look, or to augment the view.

Although it appears as if nature runs its course in the heemparks, they only exist because of constant human

Renovating the Orchideeënstuk.
Heather, Bog Asphodel, Hard Fern

intervention. No maintenance would result in a monomorphic wilderness in a short space of time. Heemparks are culture: their existence depends on their maintenance. On-going interventions are required to uphold the diversity of plants and the overall structure, a considerable difference compared to an ordinary park, which is relatively unchanging. Once such a park has been constructed very little is disturbed and the envisioned appearance is maintained as much as possible. Heemparks are dynamic in their organisation: the types of plants vary in space and time. The initial layout is but an impulse that leads to maturation, with its own dynamic and outcome. The idea of saying 'It is done' – as is known in advance with an ordinary park – does not apply to heemparks, which exist through a constant process of careful and often very subtle interventions to achieve the desired results.

Carnivorous plants

When it comes to plants, the term 'carnivorous' is a little overblown and sensationalistic. These plants rarely consume much more than small gnats and flies, so 'insect-eating' would be more appropriate. We know of roughly 630 plants that enjoy insects, divided over five families. Three groups of carnivorous plants are native to the Netherlands: the Sundew, the Blatterwort and the Butterwort.

But why do they 'eat' insects? Other ordinary plants thrive happily on water and minerals, so what is it that makes these different? The answer lies in the minerals. Carnivorous plants grow in areas where the soil has a low mineral content or where the minerals are difficult to absorb, so they supplement their diet by consuming insects. Three different types of Sundew grow in the Netherlands: the Oblong-leaved Sundew, the Round-leaved Sundew and the Great Sundew. All three attract insects with tiny droplets of sticky moisture on a stamen that imitates (morning) dew. Entrapped in the sticky mucilage, the unfortunate prey is slowly dissolved in formic acid. Sundews grow in peat lands, Round-leaved Sundews throughout the country, Oblong-leaved and Great Sundews only in the east. Great Sundew is by far the scarcest of the group.

Five types of Bladderwort grow in the Netherlands. This plant has a very special way of capturing insects. They are water plants and the only part that protrudes above the surface is the yellow flowers. It has tiny vacuum bladders and when a small aquatic insect brushes the hairs on the front of the bladder, it opens and the insect is sucked inside, where it is digested.

Butterwort is related to the Bladderwort but uses a different strategy. The leaves of this reddish-purple flowering plant slowly curl up to expose a sticky underside. A small insect landing here is dead meat. You will find Oblong-leaved and Round-leaved Sundews in several places in the parks. The Common Butterwort grows in a number of places too. The best examples, also for photographs, are in the heemplant nursery, where we have more varieties and they are easier to see. The nursery is usually open during the week between 8.00 and 16.00, and if the gate is closed, you can always ask one of our employees to unlock it for you.

Common Butterwort

Round-leaved Sundew

Sometimes exhausted plants have to be replaced, and subsided peat has to be tilled or even replaced. Experiments don't always succeed, and plants are moved to drier or moister ground, or other varieties are introduced. In this way the fundamental landscape type is preserved but each year the details in execution differ. This is why you might not find any orchids here at the moment.

Broerse wanted to create a limited form of high moorland on Het Orchideeënstuk. He scattered heads of Sphagnum on exposed, wet peat; these grew into large moss 'pillows' that retain rainwater. Moss pillows are themselves home to the mysterious Round-leaved Sundew, a carnivorous plant that ensnares small insects and spiders. Fine hair-like projections on the leaves are covered with glistening drops of a sugary substance (the 'dew') that insects find irresistible. Once an insect lands it cannot free itself and the leaf rolls up, enfolding the insect that it then digests. Lying on your stomach and looking through a macro-lens is the best way to see how beautiful the 'dewy' leaves are in the light. Equally fine are the

Small Cranberry, from a distance and close up

cyclamen-like Small Cranberry blossoms. Cranberries are enjoyed throughout northern Europe in desserts and as flavouring in alcoholic beverages. Bog Asphodel introduces some elevation to this rather downy landscape. Rare Dwarf Cornel with its red berries grows on the opposite side of the path. Some botanists regard this as a relic from the Ice Age, which would suggest that this plant decided to stay when the ice retreated. The furthest south it can be found growing in the European wild is in the Dutch province, Drenthe.

Dwarf Cornel

Wood Spurge

When you reach the convergence of the flagstone paths, turn round and walk back in the direction you came from, but now on the left path around the back of Het Orchideeënstuk. Below the canopy of leaves you will find lots of Angled Solomon's Seal and Lily-of-the-Valley. Leave Het Orchideeënstuk via the bridge and turn right towards the intersection. You are on the last short section of the Klokjespad. Blackthorn grows here, a species of prunus that produces beautiful purplish-blue berries in autumn. Commonly known as sloe, these berries are so sour that if you eat one your mouth will pucker for rest of the day. They are best enjoyed after a night or two of autumn frost and are used to make jam, or to flavour Dutch gin and brandy.

If you like, turn left into the **Viooltjespad** and take a look down this dark corridor primarily consisting of Maple, Ash, Guelder Rose, Fly Honeysuckle, June Berry and Hazel. Below them grow modestly flowering varieties such as Wood

Speedwell, Wood Spurge and Common Dog, surrounded by Brittle Bladder Fern, Hart's Tongue Fern and Dog Violet. Violets used to grow here in great numbers but the path has become overgrown and it is too dark for these exuberant little flowers. Columbine is quite at home among these shade-loving plants. This plant grows wild throughout the Netherlands. For centuries the unusual shape of its flowers has been a source of inspiration for some: the deeply religious, for example, see in the shape of the flower a dove representing the Holy Ghost; others see a dunce's cap, a sign of stupidity.

Return to the crossroads and walk along the **Bedstropad** that leads to the hill created from domestic rubbish where Landwehr occasionally hid during the war. At the beginning of this path, immediately on your right after the small bridge you will see Cowberry, Deptford Pink and Better Vetch, combined with German Greenweed and ferns. The path gently ascends towards higher and drier ground with an area of sublime design by Chris Broerse that is noteworthy for its

Dog Violet

Birches with Greater Celandine

simplicity: white birches in the middle of one specific type of
ground cover, Celandine, also called Wartwort. Its scientific
name is *Chelidonium*, Greek for 'swallow's herb'. It received
this name because it was believed that mother swallows
dropped a bit of juice from the Greater Celandine into the
eyes of their born-blind fledglings, enabling them to see.
Interestingly, it actually did have a reputation as a botanical

drug to clear the eyes and sharpen the sight. But a word of warning; the sap is so powerful that regular applications can vanquish warts, so just imagine what it could do to your eyes.

You can turn left to walk around the base of the hill first, towards the Dark Mullein and the Common Rock-Rose, which only blooms when the sun shines and the temperature is higher than 20 degrees Celcius. Here and

The hill with Butterbur, Common Rock-Rose and Dark Mullein

Butterbur

Common Rock-Rose

there on top of the hill, rare Wolfsbane towers above the rest. This member of the Buttercup family produces soft creamy-yellow flowers that resemble monk's cowls. It is the most poisonous plant in Europe, and during the Middle Ages was used to execute wrongdoers. It is not used in modern medicine. Butterbur or Umbrella Plant dominates part of this shoreline. Although beneficial in stabilising banks, this

Birthwort

beautiful ornamental plant is quite troublesome because the thick, creeping rhizome is difficult to remove. The Butterbur alongside the path is accompanied by Birthwort, which flowers in May and June. The pipe-shaped flowers have a bulbous base, and the inner part of the tube is coated with fine hairs that act as a flytrap. Insects become trapped and cannot escape. The hairs only relax after an insect is thoroughly coated with pollen or fertilisation has occurred, allowing it to flee the flower.

Now turn right at the crossroads, follow the path towards the top of the hill and pause for a moment by the benches to admire the view over the lower-lying water and the **Kamperfoeliepad** along the opposite shore. This path is particularly beautiful during spring when Wood Anemones bloom. Summer is marked by the somewhat nondescript Opposite-leaved Golden Saxifrage and Marsh Marigold. The latter prefers wet grassland close to watercourses and is avoided by livestock, as it is slightly toxic.

Beneath the trees, the Kamperfoeliepad joins up with the **Krentenbloesempad** that is connected to the exclusive residential neighbourhood around the park in the middle and at both ends. This path is primarily a green corridor of Alder, Common Beech, Large Oak and Guelder Rose with undergrowth consisting of Common Fleabane and Skullcaps. The stream alongside the path is home to ferns and small Rough Horsetail, which resembles bamboo. Its larger self grows further ahead, close to the little Heempark house, alongside the watercourse.

Descend the hill the way that you came, via the Bedstropad, into the ocean of plants on both sides that give this path its Dutch name, 'Bedstro' ('Bed straw'). The flowers spread a sweet fragrance. Sweet Woodruff was used as bedding straw in cots. Stay on this path, which takes you to the next garden room where the Spindle is the first plant you see, a beautiful shrub bearing red fruit that looks like a cardinal's hat. Most of the right side of the path is covered

Rough Horsetail

In 2008 a group of British landscape architects was given a tour of the three parks by some heempark employees. They compared weeding to grazing, and called the employees 'human grazers'. In many ways this is a good description. The diversity of herbaceous plants in nature is affected by many different conditions. Besides abiotic factors such as temperature, humidity, sunlight, and the acidity of the soil (pH value), the intensity of grazing also plays a great role, as does the types of animals doing the grazing. Rabbits eat in different way from red deer or large cattle. The weeding in the park aims to maintain the same type of diversity and even enlarge it. All the abovementioned factors – and these are just a few – determine if a plant can grow in a particular location and/or reproduce. Each variety has a specific tolerance and an optimum. As an example, let's

take the amount of zinc in the ground and the Calamine Violet. The Calamine Violet can grow in almost any type of soil, meaning it has high tolerance levels, but it thrives if there is a substantial quantity of zinc in the ground. Few plants can tolerate high levels of zinc, so in areas such as this, Calamine Violet has a significant competitive advantage, while other varieties struggle to survive, or don't manage to grow at all. This does not mean that Calamine Violets cannot grow in soil with

Calamine Violet

with Wall Germander, another variety rare in the wild. Behind it is Dusky Crane's-bill, also known as Mourning Widow, with its dark purple flowers.

You have arrived in the **Mosdal**. This section of the park was constructed in 1950 when activities that were stopped in 1942 due to the war were resumed, but the

Dusky Crane's-bill

significantly lower zinc values; instead they yield to plants that flourish in exactly those soil conditions.

Weeding out competitors enables us to grow many more types of plants in the peaty ground in the heemparks than most people would expect. Weeding – especially during the warmer half of the year – is the most important and time-consuming of all the maintenance tasks. In an ordinary public park this is done with a hoe. This method is too coarse for heemparks, so squatting staff wielding weeding knives do the work. This requires extensive knowledge of plants on the part of heempark employees, who have to be able to recognise varieties while they are still very small to ensure that they don't end up in the compost.

original idea of building luxurious residences on the entire Westelijke Bovenlanden had been postponed. The Second World War compounded the need for housing, but the number of people who could afford a luxury house had declined significantly. So a lot of Duplex houses were built, as can clearly be seen along the Emmakade and Mauritslaan at the back of the Dr. Koos Landwehrpark. Only one-third of the intended villas were built on the west side of the Amsterdamseweg. The spaces between were used for temporary playing fields, with three football pitches. The old historic strip of peat-and-reed land along the southward Hoornsloot was added to the first section of the heempark and a large lake was dug, the result of a pragmatic concession

Ivy-leaved Bellflower

by Broerse who used the excavated ground to elevate the
playing fields.

The Mosdal – 'Moss Valley' – is named after the peat
moss (Spaghnum) that grows in the four peat holes in this
garden room. They are populated by a multitude of small,
scarce plants, which are too delicate to allow visitors access to
the downy pillows of peat. Special varieties such as
Chaffweed, Allseed, Yellow Centaury and Oblong-leaved
Sundew are cultivated in micro-environment basins in the
nursery in De Braak. Three very rare plants grow around the
edges of the peat holes. Like the Dwarf Cornel, the Bearberry
is probably a relic from the Ice Age. It only grows in the wild
on the island Terschelling. The Lesser Skullcap is also rare in
the wild. Here, though, it has to be regularly thinned out to
make room for varieties that would otherwise perish, like
Round-leaved Sundew, Chaffweed, Yellow Centaury and
Butterwort. Finally, admire the Ivy-leaved Bellflower, already
extinct in the wild in 1959.

There is a likelihood that if you look around you – in this garden room and elsewhere in the parks – that you mostly see only dark soil and not the scenes described in this book. This is because the layer of peat on which you are walking is just as dynamic as the communities of plant that grow on it. The peat ground is naturally preserved when the groundwater level is high enough that oxygen cannot decompose the peat. In areas where the water level falls, the peat layer perishes, so to forestall this it is elevated regularly. This is mostly done during the winter months. The dead upper layer is replaced with a layer of fresh peat, gathered in areas being prepared for housing developments. But working with peat is complicated, as it can differ considerably. The nutrient values depend on the origin of the peat. Places where the peat develops under the influence of groundwater will have more nourishment (low moorland) than places where it only develops under the influence of rainwater (high moorland). When construction of the three heemparks began, the upper layer of peat was decayed.

Coral Necklace

Bog Asphodel in spring and autumn

Broerse turned the ground on its head: the top layer ended up at the bottom, and the fresh, pristine peat from below was placed on top. The plants in all three parks had to adjust to the peat – either by habituation or, as just mentioned, by weeding out competitors. In a few places Broerse introduced clay or muddy sand, to create conditions for other types of plants, as you will see later on in the description of the Margrietenpad. The Mosdal has only high moorland peat, with its characteristic low plants, beautifully garnished in the peat holes with Bog Asphodel, flowering yellow in June and producing lovely orange-red fruit in autumn. For many years, people believed that this plant made the bones of livestock porous if they ate it, because Bog Asphodel grows in mineral-poor, acidic peat with very little calcium. Livestock grazing in meadows with this plant therefore had too little calcium in their diets, making their bones brittle and more prone to breakage. More likely is that this plant only grows in soggy ground, into which large animals can easily sink. Bog Asphodel only grows in wet and

Primroses

All three types of primrose found in the Netherlands also grow in our parks: the Wild Primrose, the Oxlip and the Cowslip Primrose. In the Netherlands primroses are better known by their scientific name *Primula*, which means 'first born' (this is often the first plant to flower in the woods). People used to eat them – in jams and salads as well as in cakes and pancakes. It is used as an herbal remedy to treat coughs. In the parks we try to separate the three types because they so easily cross-pollinate, even with cultivated varieties growing in gardens adjacent to the parks. The Wild Primrose blooms the earliest with soft yellow flowers on short stalks. Ants cannot resist the oily seed coats, thereby helping with propagation. The Oxlip has sprigs of light yellow flowers on long stalks; it flowers early and the blooms usually pend towards one side. It prefers a light shady place and no additional fertiliser. The Cowslip Primrose has much darker, yolk-yellow flowers, also on stalks, but the flowers droop on all sides. Of the three, Cowslip Primrose is most fond of the sun. Cowslips are known by several other names, including St. Peter's Keys, Herb Peter, and Keys of Heaven, derived from the story of St. Peter, who fell asleep at the Gates to Heaven and dropped his keys. The place where they landed was where the first Cowslips grew.

Primrose

Birches with Yellow Anemone, Oxlip and Dog Violet

acidic areas to the east and south of the Netherlands. The widespread exploitation of the Netherlands has made it a scarce and now a protected species. The low profile of this garden room is punctuated by the immense Regal Ferns on both side of the water, itself home to water lilies that add a touch of romance to this view.

After crossing a little bridge, the Mosdal becomes the Veenbespad, which takes you through a birch grove. In spring the perimeter of this is coloured pale yellow by Cowslip Primrose. This blends perfectly with the blues of the various types of violets. Lily-of-the-Valley also blooms here later in the year. Looking closely at the birches you will notice that some of the trunks have a kink at eye height. Shortly after the saplings were

Great Fen Sedge

Yellow Water Lily

planted in 1987, an energetic
but misguided vandal broke a
dozen or so treetops. They
managed to survive and
sprouted new branches just
below the fracture, which grew
upwards. The only trace of this
dastardly deed is a slight bend
in the trunks, a scar marking
their mutilation years ago.

Leaving the birch grove and following the **Veenbespad** brings
you to another garden room, which includes one end of the
large lake Broerse had dug so he could use the excavated ground
to elevate the land beneath the playing fields. At your right is a
peat moor with a diversity of plants around its shore. The water
near the benches with view over the Hoornsloot and the

Amsterdamse Bos on the opposite side is home to Great Fen Sedge, a member of the Cypress Grass family. Feel the edges of the serrated and razor sharp bluish-green leaves, but do take care not to cut your fingers. Preferable, perhaps, is rubbing leaves of the Wild Marjoram that grows beside the bench on the right to release its fragrance, which is reminiscent of the widely cultivated and used herb, Oregano. Brandybottle, the national plant of Friesland, drifts in the water. After its yellow blooms have finished flowering, the seedpods float on the water surface, revealing the reason for their English name – they look just like the small green bottles once used for brandy. Alongside them is Lesser Bulrush with its familiar cigar-shaped spike.

The left side of the path is lined with high peat land that supports heather and Tundra Bilberry, recognisable from its blue-green leaves. As the path disappears into a grove of birch trees, Hard Fern comes into view. It produces two types of fronds: the sterile horizontal fronds do not produce spores, which only appear on the thinner upright, fertile fronds. Most of the lake is visible from beneath the trees; the plant after which this path is named is in the foreground: the Cranberry. Originally from North America, it was brought to the

Cranberry

View over the large lake during winter

Netherlands in 1840. A beachcomber on Terschelling found it in a barrel on the beach, but discovering that it held sour red berries and not wine, he left it in the dunes. It was from here that birds spread the seeds across north and west Netherlands and Drenthe. On Terschelling the fruit is still harvested to

make stewed fruit, jam and juice. A link between peat land and dipsomania is again confirmed by the Sweet Flag that grow on the banks here. Probably originating in South-East Asia, extracts from the rootstock have been used for generations in the Netherlands to flavour food and drinks such as the Dutch spice cake, 'Deventer koek', and Berenburg, a Dutch alcoholic drink.

Leaving the Veenbespad via the small bridge, at the fork you have to walk along a small section of the **Margrietenpad** that veers left around the lake and passes the sports fields, to end at the exclusive neighbourhood. Especially noticeable is the Great Burnet, which blooms from June to September, its dark red flowerheads without petals. They look a little like a croquette on a stick. The leaves are added to salads. In spring Snakes Head Frittelary makes an appearance, especially close to the Regal Ferns. It grows well here because the ground around the base of the ferns is bare and Frittelary flowers before the fern fronds have fully unfurled.

Cornfield flowers

In summer your gaze will invariably fall upon the little field to the right of the path. Plants here do not have to adapt to the peat, but the other way round. A layer of sand is regularly deposited here and each year it is dug over and sown with cornfield flowers. These are plants that have grown in fields between grain since time immemorial and which are regarded as pests because they are harvested along with the crop, resulting in impure grain with sometimes-toxic components. Flour with traces of Corn Cockle, for example, caused stomach and intestinal problems. Like Poppy and Cornflower, this limp, slouching plant is supported by the grain stalks, but modern farming techniques and the use of

Stinsplants

A '*stins*' is a former fortified farmhouse in the province of Friesland, the Netherlands, usually owned by noblemen or prominent citizens. In 1932 the Dutch term 'stinsenplanten' ('stinsplants') was applied for the first time to a group of plant varieties originally planted by humans but which, over the years, went feral on stinses, rural estates, farmsteads and in gardens. All stinsplants are herbaceous plants. Most of them are bulbous, tuberous or rootstock plants, but there are also plenty that fall outside these categories. Most flower in spring, but again, there are exceptions. Many were brought from abroad, but some have always been here. In brief, determining a clear definition of what a stinsplant is and what is not is no simple task. The best-known stinsplants are various species of Snowdrop, Crocus, Bluebell, Daffodil, Hyacinth, Fritillary and Anemone. This list in itself conveys the differences: Fritillary, Narcissus and Wood Anemone are naturally occurring plants in the Netherlands, which made the journey over the hedge from the wild into gardens. The long-established cultivation of other varieties compounds the difficulty in establishing if they are indigenous. Snowdrops are thought to have still been growing wild in only one location in the Achterhoek (a predominately rural area in the eastern part of the Netherlands) until 1916. It still grows on

Fritillary

Wood Anemone

some farms. The origins of the Wild Daffodil have long been disputed, but now we believe that it is indigenous to the Netherlands. The first records of the Star-of-Bethlehem and the Wild Tulip date to 1770, so these can definitely be considered as indigenous to the Netherlands. The various types of Lungwort, Giant Bellflower, and Dusky Crane's-bill are interesting examples. These are not typical bulbous plants – the Giant Bellflower even blooms during the summer. Many stinsplants come from mountains in Central European or from Turkey.

Wealthy merchants even financed expeditions to collect new varieties of stinsplants and bring them to the Netherlands. The story behind the English Bluebell is quite special. It was first recorded in the Netherlands in around 1700. It is believed that the plant was brought here from England, which at the time had the same king as the Netherlands (William III from the House of Orange), obviously resulting in much interaction between the two countries between 1688 and 1702.

View over the large lake with Purple Loosestrife and Meadowsweet

pure grain types have compounded its scarcity. Some weeds manage to endure though, including the Tuberous Pea, a variety of the genus *Lathyrus* that produces radical tubers. These survive the harvest and ploughing to once again raise their green heads in spring. Many cornfield flowers are truly beautiful: few plants can equal the deep blue of Blue Pimpernel, the purplish-blue of Forking Larkspur, or the blood-red of a Poppy. Corn Marigold and the white-blooming Sneezewort are beautiful interlopers. At the nursery these cornfield flowers are sown in tidy rows so that their seeds can be easily collected for the following year.

The other side of the path has a glorious view over the lake. Further on, the Margrietenpad is particularly beautiful in spring when the early flowering Spring Snowflake

Sneezewort

View from the entrance on the Prinses Irenelaan

blooms. This bulbous plant could be found on the Tanken-
berg, a nature reserve in Twente, until 1916 but now is only
seen as a domesticated stinsplant. On the shore on the right
hand side of the bench, Purple Loosestrife blooms from June
to September with long spikes of pink flowers. Interspersed

with these are the green umbels of the Marsh Spurge: these examples are descendants of plants that once grew in the reed-lands of Amstelveense Poel. A little further ahead you encounter Whorled Solomon's Seal that turns a vibrant straw-yellow in autumn. If you continue along this path you can leave the park, but you might not want to just yet.

Return to the intersection with the Veenbespad and continue along the **Hazelaarpad** when you get to the fork. A Bracken-lined path brings you to a little patch of Molinia meadow on the left that is similar to the one in the Dr. Koos Landwehrpark. Before the invention of artificial fertilisers in the early twentieth century, grasslands such as this abounded in the Netherlands, for example, in the agrarian landscape in the east of the country. All year round sheep grazed on the heaths and when they were stabled during winter they were fed hay from the same patches of Molinia meadow. The dung from the flock was mixed with sods of peat and used to fertilise the villages' farmlands. Mowing the grasslands meant the soil remained poor and sustained communities of plants consisting of

Common Reed

Autumn Crocus

Greater Tussock Sedge

now-rare varieties. This little patch of meadow in the park is not fertilised either – it is mown twice yearly with a scythe. The grass is heavily populated by Devil's-bit Scabious, Greater Yellow Rattle, Southern Marsh-orchid, Broad-leaved Marsh-orchid, Lesser Butterfly-orchid, Brown Knapweed and especially Whorled Caraway. This plant is extinct in the wild in our country, but still grows in one place in Amsterdam, probably because its seeds were scattered there. Along the shore, Greater Tussock Sedge is visible. The Autumn Crocus blooms with pink, Crocus-like flowers on the other side of the path in the season from which it takes part of its name. This plant is unrelated to the Crocus; its name refers to the unusual time that the flower opens. Its leaves only appear in spring, as do the poisonous seedpods with seeds that rattle audibly if you shake them.

Hazelaarpad with German Greenweed and Dark Mullein

In bygone days children picked the seedpods and played with them. Some ate the seeds, which contain the toxin colchicine. Eating only five seeds is fatal, yet colchicine is an anti-inflammatory agent that in very modest quantities has been used to treat gout and, more recently, cancer.

The area around the bench in this garden room is home to several types of grass, including Wood Millet and False Brome. Hollowroot is profuse here in spring, its flowers tinted purple, white and an in-between colour that florist and heempark pioneer Sipkes called 'like a lady's knickers'. And indeed, park

employees still refer to this plant as 'the one with the old-fashioned ladies' knickers colour'.

Now you are at a T-junction – this time with the Gentianenpad on the left and the Jeneverbespad on the right. Bram Galjaard, who succeeded Chris Broerse as director of Amstelveen's Parks and Public Gardens Department in 1967, constructed this section of the park between 1970 and 1972. It is a relatively small area of land and had to be given as broad a perspective as possible to mask the unsightly view over the backyards of the houses on the Oude Karselaan. Part of the ditch at the back was filled in and a 'terrestialised shore' was

Jeneverbespad

constructed here that was intended to show the entire development of marsh flora in its successive stages. This was the final section of the Thijssepark.

Turn right along the **Jeneverbespad**, named after the juniper ('jenever' in Dutch) bushes planted here and there. Juniper bushes are one of the few naturally occurring conifers in the Benelux. The lime-rich edges of the path are a profusion of Wood Spurge, a poisonous banishing herb with greenish-yellow flowers, and the yellow-flowering St. John's Wort.

Marsh Gentian

Return to the intersection and proceed along the **Gentianen-pad,** named after the blue Marsh Gentian that grows here. You will see Plantain-leaved Leopard's Bane on your left, just before the inter-section. Ahead – you have to bend down to see it – is a tiny plant called Parsley-piert; its leaves are redolent of parsley. Like many other rare varieties, this plant originates

Parasites and semi-parasites

Parasites are plants and animals that survive off other plants or animals without symbiosis. Our parks are home to parasites and semi-parasites. Parasites do not produce chlorophyll and extract all their nourishment from the roots of their host. Semi-parasites do photosynthesise and only rely on their host for water and minerals. The Yellow Rattle is a semi-parasite that lives off several varieties of grass. Humans in the past used it for exactly this purpose: Rattles were sown to reduce the number of times a field had to be scythed. Ivy Broomrape grows in the vicinity of the banishing pole in De Braak and close to the Heempark house in the Thijssepark. The roots of this leafless parasite draw nourishment from Ivy. Purple Toothwort, an especially beautiful parasite, grows along the Gentianenpad in the Thijssepark and in huge quantities along the Drijvend Pad in De Braak. In spring the salvia-like purple flowers seem to appear from nowhere and cover large areas before vanishing as quickly as they materialised.

Ivy Broomrape

in Limburg. We did not plant it here, so it must have arrived with other plants from our nursery, but it's obviously quite happy and complements the view. Also a ground-hugger is the parasite Purple Toothwort, which grows beneath certain types of shrubs and trees – preferably willows – and draws its nourishment from the roots of its host. It does not develop an

Tomasini's Crocus

aboveground stem and its purple flowers poke through the
surface directly from the rootstock between March and May.
Crosswort, slightly further along, is characterised by its square
stalks with groups of four soft downy leaves, arranged
crosswise in a whorl. Yellow flowers grow just above the leaves
between April and June. Scattered about is the by now familiar
Bog Asphodel, with Marsh Cinquefoil lining the ditch.

At the end of the Gentianenpad turn left over a short bridge
and follow the water past the playing fields onto the
Spaanderspad. In early spring – as early as March, even –
this area is a profusion of Tomasini's Crocuses that produce
a carpet of pink blooms. Tomasini's Crocus is a stinsplant
originating in the Balkans. During summer this area is a
medley of different plants and colours. Brown Knapweed and
Soapwort are irresistible eye-catchers. Soapwort, with its
creamy-pink flowers, is named for the poisonous saponins in
its roots. Boiled with water, its leaves can be beaten to a foamy
liquid that can be used to bleach washing. The Sea Buckthorn

Kornoeljepad with Common Pellitory in the foreground

is especially lovely in autumn, when these prickly shrubs –
which grow in profusion in dune lands – yield bright orange
berries. In winter the berries can ferment and the birds that eat
them – starlings and thrushes – become drunk and struggle to
fly. Two members of the family of labiates also catch the eye:
the first is purple-flowering Betony or Bishop's Wort. In olden
days it was a widely used emetic and coagulant and was also
used to treat fevers. Nowadays Betony is used to treat bronchial
complaints, diarrhoea and bladder infections. Originally from
Central Asia, the second labiate, Motherwort, now grows
throughout the world. It is used as an herb in cooking and, in
days gone by, in beer; it has also seen years of use as a remedy
for heart ailments and muscle cramp.

The Spaanderspad ends at the **Rode Kornoeljepad**, a green corridor that leads to the park exit. Oxlip and Tomasini's Crocus bloom around the intersection in spring. Take a few steps to right to see Common Pellitory, a sizeable perennial herb with unremarkable flowers from Central and Southern Europe. It grows along the right hand side of the path. In all likelihood it arrived with the Romans, who used it as medicine; it appears to be an excellent agent to polish glasses as well. Agrimony blooms here happily from June to August with yellow flowers on a long spike. Return to the intersection and continue along the path towards the exit past the Rough Chervil's white umbels. If cows eat too much of this they behave as if intoxicated – it is slightly poisonous. Its leaves bear similarities to genuine chervil, but these two types are unrelated. In the background, Dwarf Alder, which blooms in July and August with reddish-white flowers that smell like bitter almonds.

You have reached the exit and are now standing on Amsterdamseweg, less than 100 metres from the Banpaal in De Braak. We hope you have enjoyed your experience. But before we bid you farewell, one final suggestion: take another stroll along these paths in a different season and see how much you recognise. Here, some things change almost every week.

Betony

List of plant names

Agrimony	Agrimonia eupatoria
Alder	Alnus glutinosa
Alder Buckthorn	Rhamnus frangula
Allseed	Radiola linoides
Alternate-leaved Golden Saxifrage	Chrysosplenium alternifolium
American Cranberry	Vaccinium macrocarpon
Angled Solomon's Seal	Polygonatum odoratum
Apple	Malus sylvestris
Arnica	Arnica montana
Arrowhead	Sagittaria sagittifolia
Ash	Fraxinus excelsior
Aspen	Populus tremula
Autumn Crocus	Colchicum autumnale
Barberry	Berberis vulgaris
Basil Thyme	Clinopodium acinos
Bay Willow	Salix pentandra
Bearberry	Arctostaphylos uva-ursi
Beech Fern	Phegoteris connectilis
Bell Heather	Erica cinerea
Berry Catchfly	Silene baccifer
Betony	Stachys officinalis
Bilberry	Vaccinium myrtillus
Bird Cherry	Prunus padus
Bird-in-a-bush	Corydalis solida
Birthwort	Aristolochia clematitis
Bistort	Polygonum bistorta
Bitter Vetch	Lathyrus linifolius
Bittersweet Nightshade	Solanum dulcamara
Black Elder	Sambucus nigra
Black Horehound	Ballota nigra subsp. meridionalis
Black Poplar	Populus nigra
Black-horned Rampion	Phyteuma spicatum subsp. nigrum
Blackthorn	Prunus spinosa
Bladder Campion	Silene vulgaris
Blue Pimpernel	Anagallis arvensis subsp. foemina
Bog Arum	Calla palustris
Bog Asphodel	Narthecium ossifragum
Bog Bilberry	Vaccinium uliginosum
Bog Myrtle	Myrica gale
Bog Pimpernel	Anagallis tenella
Bog-rosemary	Andromeda polifolia
Bogbean	Menyanthes trifoliata
Bracken	Pteridium aquilinum
Branched Bur-reed	Sparganium erectum
Brittle Bladder Fern	Cystopteris fragilis
Broad Buckler Fern	Dryopteris dilatata
Broad-leaved Helleborine	Epipactis helleborine subsp. helleborine
Broad-leaved Marsh-orchid	Dactylorhiza majalos supsp. majalis
Broad-leaved Ragwort	Senecio sarracenicus
Brookweed	Samolus valerandi
Brown Knapweed	Centaurea jacea
Buckthorn	Rhamnus cathartica
Bulrush	Typha latifolia
Burnet	Sanguisorba minor
Burnet Rose	Rosa pimpinellifolia
Butterbur	Petasites hybridus

Cabbage Thistle	Cirsium oleraceum
Calamine Violet	Viola lutea subsp.calaminaria
Carpet Bugle	Ajuga reptans
Carthusian Pink	Dianthus carthusianorum
Chaffweed.	Centunculus minimus
Chestnut Oak	Quercus petraea
Chicory	Cichorium intybus
Cinnamon Rose	Rosa majalis
Climbing Corydalis	Ceratocapnos claviculata
Clustered Bellflower	Campanula glomerata
Columbine	Aquilegia vulgaris
Common Beech	Fagus sylvatica
Common Beech	Carpinus betulus
Common Butterwort	Pinguicula vulgaris
Common Centaury	Centaurium erythraea
Common Club-rush	Schoenoplectus lacustris
Common Comfrey	Symphytum officinale
Common Cottongrass	Eriophorum angustifolium
Common Dandelion	Taraxacum officinale
Common Dog Violet	Viola riviniana
Common Figwort	Scrophularia nodosa
Common Fleabane	Pulicaria dysenterica
Common Foxglove	Digitalis purpurea
Common Gromwell	Lithospermum officinale
Common Holly	Ilex aquifolium
Common Hop	Humulus lupulus
Common Horsetail	Equisetum arvense
Common Ivy	Hedera helix
Common Juniper	Juniperus communis
Common Meadow-rue	Thalictrum flavum
Common Pellitory	Parietaria officinalis
Common Ragwort	Jacobaea vulgaris subsp. vulgaris
Common Reed	Phragmites australis
Common Restharrow	Ononis repens
Common Rock-Rose	Helianthemum nummularium
Common Scurvy-grass	Cochlearia officinalis
Common Sorrel	Rumex acetosa
Common Stonecrop	Sedum acre
Common Tansy	Tanacetum vulgare
Common Valerian	Valeriana officinalis
Common Vincetoxicum	Vincetoxicum hirundinaria
Common Water-plantain	Alisma plantago-aquatica
Common Wintergreen	Pyrola minor
Compact Grape Hyacinth	Muscari botryoides
Coral Necklace	Illecebrum verticillatum
Corn Cockle	Agrostemma githago
Corn Marigold	Glebionis segetum
Cornflower	Centaurea cyanus
Cotton Thistle	Onopordum acanthium
Cow Parsley	Anthriscus silvestris
Cowbane	Cicuta virosa
Cowberry	Vaccinium vitis-idaea
Cowherb	Vaccaria hispanica
Cowslip	Primula veris
Cranberry	Vaccinium macrocarpon
Creeping Bellflower	Campanula rapunculoides
Creeping Jenny	Lysimachia nummularia
Creeping Willow	Salix repens
Crested Buckler Fern	Dryopteris cristata
Cross-leaved Gentian	Gentiana cruciata
Cross-Leaved Heath	Erica tetralix
Crosswort	Galium cruciata

Crowberry	Empetrum nigrum
Crown Vetch	Coronilla varia
Cuckooflower	Cardamine pratensis
Cypress Spurge	Euphorbia cyparissias
Dark Mullein	Verbascum nigrum
Deadly Nightshade	Atropa bella-donna
Dense-flowered Mullein	Verbascum densiflorum
Deptford Pink	Dianthus armeria
Devil's-bit Scabious	Succisa pratensis
Dog Rose	Rosa canina
Dog's Mercury	Mercurialis perennis
Downy Birch	Betula pubescens
Downy Hemp Nettle	Galeopsis segetum
Drooping Star of Bethlehem	Ornithogalum nutans
Dusky Crane's-bill	Geranium phaeum
Dwarf Cornel	Cornus suecica
Dwarf Elder	Sambucus ebulus
Dwarf Periwinkle	Vinca minor
Dyer's Greenweed	Genista tinctoria
Early Dog Violet	Viola reichenbachiana
Enchanter's Nightshade	Circaea lutetiana
English Bluebell	Hyacinthoides non-scripta
Eyebright	Euphrasia stricta
Fairy Flax	Linum catharticum
False Brome	Brachypodium sylvaticum
Fen Ragwort	Jacobaea paludosa
Field Garlic	Allium vineale
Field Maple	Acer campestre
Field Mouse-ear	Cerastium arvense
Field Rose	Rosa arvensis
Field Scabious	Knautia arvensis
Flowering Rush	Butomus umbellatus
Fly Honeysuckle	Lonicera xylosteum
Forking Larkspur	Consolida regalis
Fragrant Agrimony	Agrimonia procera
Fragrant Orchid	Gymnadenia conopsea subsp.conopsea
Fritillary	Fritillaria meleagris
Frogbit	Hydrocharis morsus-ranea
Garlic Mustard	Alliaria officinalis
German Greenweed	Genista germanica L
Germander Speedwell	Veronica chamaedrys
Giant Bellflower	Campanula latifolia
Goldenrod	Solidago virgaurea
Goldilocks Buttercup	Ranunculus auricomus
Gooseberry	Ribes uva-crispa
Gorse	Ulex europaeus
Grass of Parnassus	Parnassia palustris
Gratiola	Gratiola officinalis
Great Burnet	Sanguisorba officinalis
Great Fen Sedge	Cladium mariscus
Great Horsetail	Equisetum telmateia
Great Pond Sedge	Carex riparia
Great Sundew	Drosera anglica
Greater Bladderwort	Utricularia vulgaris
Greater Celandine	Chelidonium majus
Greater Knapweed	Centaurea scabiosa
Greater Musk-mallow	Malva alcea
Greater Spearwort	Ranunculus lingua

Greater Tussock Sedge	Carex paniculata
Green Hellebore	Helleborus viridis
Grey Alder	Alnus incana
Grey Poplar	Populus x canescens
Grey Willow	Salix cinerea
Guelder Rose	Viburnum opulus
Hairy Brome	Bromopsis ramosa subsp. ramosa
Hairy Greenweed	Genista pilosa
Hairy St. John's Wort	Hypericum hirsutum
Hairy Violet	Viola hirta
Hairy Wood-rush	Luzula pilosa
Hard Fern	Blechnum spicant
Hard Shield Fern	Polystichum acculeatum
Hare's-tail Cottongrass	Eriophorum vaginatum
Harebell	Campanula rotundifolia
Hart's Tongue Fern	Asplenium scolopendrium
Hautbois Strawberry	Fragaria moschata
Hawthorn	Crataegus monogyna
Hazel	Corylus avellana
Heath Dog Violet	Viola canina
Heather	Calluna vulgaris
Hedge Bindweed	Calystegia sepium
Hedge Woundwort	Stachys sylvatica
Hedgerow Crane's-bill	Geranium pyrenaicum
Hemp Agrimony	Eupatorium cannabinum
Herb Christopher	Actaea spicata
Herb Paris	Paris quadrifolia
Herb Robert	Geranium robertianum
Highbush Blueberry	Vaccinium corymbosum
Hoary Alyssum	Berteroa incana
Hoary Cinquefoil	Potentilla argentea
Hoary Plantain	Plantago media
Hoary Ragwort	Jacobaea erucifolia
Hollowroot	Corydalis cava
Honeysuckle	Lonicera peryclimenum
Imperforate St. John's Wort	Hypericum maculatum subsp. obtusiusculum
Irish Fleabane	Inula salicina
Ivy Broomrape	Orobanche hederae
Ivy-leaved Bellfower	Wahlenbergia hederacea
Ivy-leaved Toadflax	Cymbalaria muralis
Juneberry	Amelanchier lamarckii
Lady Fern	Athyrium filix-femina
Large Bittercress	Cardamine amara
Large Skullcap	Scutellaria columnae
Large Speedwell	Veronica austriaca subsp. teucrium
Large Venus's-looking-glass	Legousia speculum-veneris
Leopard's Bane	Doronicum pardalianches
Lesser Bulrush	Typha angustifolia
Lesser Butterfly-orchid	Platanthera bifolia
Lesser Celandine	Ranunculus ficaria
Lesser Meadow-rue	Thalictrum minus
Lesser Skullcap	Scutellaria minor
Lesser Spearwort	Ranunculus flammula
Lily-of-the-Valley	Convallaria majalis
Limestone Fern	Gymnocarpium robertianum
Long-leaf Speedwell	Veronica longifolia
Lords-and-Ladies	Arum maculatum

Lungwort	Pulmonaria officinalis
Magellan's Sphagnum	Sphagnum spec.
Maiden Pink	Dianthus deltoides
Maidenhair Spleenwort	Asplenium trichomanes
Male Fern	Dryopteris filix-mas
March Gentian	Gentiana pneumonanthe
March Mallow	Althaea officinalis
Marsh Arrowgrass	Triglochin palustris
Marsh Cinquefoil	Comarum palustre
Marsh Fern	Thelypteris palustris
Marsh Hedge Nettle	Stachys palustris
Marsh Helleborine	Epipactis palustris
Marsh Lousewort	Pedicularis palustris
Marsh Marigold	Caltha palustris
Marsh Spurge	Euphorbia palustris
Marsh St. Johns Wort	Hypericum elodes
Marsh Thistle	Cirsium palustre
Marsh Valerian	Valeriana dioica
Marsh Violet	Viola palustris
May Lily	Maianthemum bifolium
Meadow Buttercup	Ranunculus acris
Meadow Clary	Salvia pratensis
Meadow Crane's-bill	Geranium pratense
Meadow Salsify	Tragopogon pratensis
Meadow Saxifrage	Saxifraga granulata
Meadow Saxifrage 'flore pleno'	Saxifraga granulata 'Plena'
Meadow Thistle	Cirsium dissectum
Meadowsweet	Filipendula ulmaria
Medlar	Mespilus germanica
Mezereon	Daphne mezereum
Midland Hawthorn	Crataegus laevigata
Milk Parsley	Peucedanum palustre
Moschatel	Adoxa moschatellina
Moss Rockbrake	Polytrichum spec.
Moth Mullein	Verbascum blattaria
Motherwort	Leonurus cardiaca
Mountain Melick	Melica nutans
Mountain Tobacco	Arnica Montana
Musk Mallow	Malva moschata
Musk Thistle	Carduus nutans
Narrow-leaved Everlasting Pea	Lathyrus sylvestris
Narrow-leaved Lungwort	Pulmonaria montana
Nettle-leaved Bellflower	Campanula trachelium
Nottingham Catchfly	Silene nutans
Oak Fern	Gymnocarpium dryopteris
Oblong-leaved Sundew	Drosera intermedia
Opposite-leaved Golden Saxifrage	Chrysosplenium oppositifolium
Orphine	Sedum telephium
Oxeye Daisy	Leucanthemum vulgare
Oxlip	Primula elatior
Pale Corydalis	Pseudofumaria alba
Pale St. John's Wort	Hypericum montanum
Parsley piert	Aphanes australis
Parsnip	Pastinaca sativa
Pasqueflower	Pulsatilla vulgaris
Peach-leaved Bellflower	Campanula persicifolia
Pear	Pyrus communis
Pedunculate Oak	Quercus robur

Pellitory-of-the-Wall	Parietaria judaica
Pendulous Sedge	Carex pendula
Pennyroyal	Mentha pulegium
Perfoliate Alexanders	Smyrnium perfoliatum
Perforate St. John's Wort	Hypericum perforatum
Petty Whin	Genista anglica
Plantain-leaved Leopard's Bane	Doronicum plantagineum
Polypody	Polypodium vulgare
Primrose	Primula vulgaris
Proliferous Pink	Petrorhagia prolifera
Purple Chokeberry	Aronia x prunifolia
Purple Loosestrife	Lythrum salicaria
Purple Toothwort	Lathraea clandestina
Ragged Robin	Lychnis flos-cuculi
Rampion Bellflower	Campanula rapunculus
Red Campion	Silene dioica
Red Currants	Ribes rubrum
Red Dogwood	Cornus sanguinea
Red-berried Elder	Sambucus racemosa
Reflexed Stonecrop	Sedum reflexum
Regal Fern	Osmunda regalis
Rosebay Willow-herb	Chamerion angustifolium
Rough Chervil	Chaerophyllum temulum
Rough Horsetail	Equisetum hyemale
Round-leaved Mint	Mentha suaveolens
Round-leaved Sundew	Drosera rotundifolia
Round-leaved Wintergreen	Pyrola rotundifolia
Rowan	Sorbus aucuparia
Salsify	Tragopogon porrifolius
Sand Leek	Allium scorodoprasum
Sanicle	Sanicula europaea
Sarcococca	Sarcococca hookeriana
Saw-wort	Serratula tinctoria
Scotch Broom	Cytisus scoparius
Scotch Mist	Galium sylvaticum
Sea Buckthorn	Hippophae rhamnoides
Sea Kale	Crambe martima
Selfheal	Prunella vulgaris
Shallon	Gaultheria shallon
Sheep's Bit	Jasione montana
Shoreweed	Littorella uniflora
Silver Berch	Betula pendula
Slender St. John's Wort	Hypericum pulchrum
Small Cranberry	Vaccinium oxycoccus
Small Scabious	Scabiosa columbaria
Small Teasel	Dipsacus pilosa
Small-flowered Catchfly	Silene gallica
Small-leaved Sweet Briar	Rosa agrestis
Sneezewort	Achillea ptarmica
Snowdrop	Galanthus nivalis
Soapwort	Saponaria officinalis
Soft Downy-rose	Rosa villosa
Soft Rush	Juncus effusus
Solomon's Seal	Polygonatum multiflorum
Southern Marsh-orchid	Dactylorhiza majalis subsp. praetermissa
Spiked Rampion	Phyteuma spicatum subsp. spicatum
Spindle	Euonymus europaeus
Spiny Restharrow	Ononis spinosa
Spotted Dead Nettle	Lamium maculatum
Spotted Hawkweed	Hieracium maculatum

Spring Snowflake	Leucojum vernum
Square-stalked St. John's Wort	Hypericum tetrapterum
Star of Bethlehem	Ornithogalum umbellatum
Stichwort	Stellaria holostea
Summer Snowflake	Leucojum aestivum
Sweet Briar	Rosa rubiginosa
Sweet Cherry	Prunus avium
Sweet Flag	Acorus calamus
Sweet Vernal Grass	Anthoxanthum odoratum
Sweet Violet	Viola odorata
Sweet Woodruff	Galium odoratum
Tasteless Stonecrop	Sedum sexangulare
Taxodium	Taxodium distichum
Tomasini's Crocus	Crocus tommasinianus
Tower Mustard	Arabis glabra
Trailing St. John's Wort	Hypericum humifusum
Traveler's Joy	Clematis vitalba
Tuberous Pea	Lathyrus tuberosus
Twinflower	Linnaea borealis
Upland Enchanter's Nightshade	Circea x intermedia
Vervain	Verbena officinalis
Viper's Buglos	Echium vulgare
Wall Germander	Teucrium chamaedrys
Water Avens	Geum rivale
Water Forget-me-not	Myosotis scorpioides subsp. scorpioides
Water Germander	Teucrium scordium
Water Mint	Mentha aquatica
Water Soldier	Stratiotes aloides
Weasel's-snout	Misopates orontium
White Bryony	Bryonia dioica
White Stonecrop	Sedum album
White Water Lily	Nymphaea alba
White Willow	Salix alba
White Wood-rush	Luzula luzuloides
Whorled Caraway	Carum verticillatum
Whorled Clary	Salvia verticillata
Whorled Solomon's Seal	Polygonatum verticillatum
Wild Angelica	Angelica sylvestris
Wild Daffodil	Narcissus pseudonarcissus subsp. pseudonarcissus
Wild Garlic	Allium ursinum
Wild Liquorice	Astragalus glycyphyllos
Wild Marjoram	Origanum vulgare
Wild Pansy	Viola tricolor
Wild Privet	Ligustrum vulgare
Wild Strawberry	Fragaria vesca
Wild Teasel	Dipsacus fullonum
Wild Thyme	Thymus serpyllum
Wild Tulip	Tulipa sylvestris
Woad	Isatis tinctoria
Wolf's Bane	Aconitum vulparia
Wood Anemone	Anemone nemorosa
Wood Buttercup	Ranunculuc polyanthemos subsp. nemorosus
Wood Horsetail	Equisetum sylvaticum
Wood Melick	Melica uniflora
Wood Millet	Milium effusum
Wood Ragwort	Senecio nemorensis

Wood Sage	Teucrium scorodonia
Wood Sorrel	Oxalis acetosella
Wood Speedwell	Veronica montana
Wood Spurge	Euphorbia amygdaloides
Wood Stitchwort	Stellaria nemorum
Woolly Thistle	Cirsium eriophorum
Yarrow	Achillea millefolium
Yellow Anemone	Anemone ranunculoides
Yellow Archangel	Lamiastrum galeobdolon subsp. galeobdolon
Yellow Bedstraw	Galium verum
Yellow Centaury	Cicendia filiformis
Yellow Corydalis	Pseudofumaria lutea
Yellow Figwort	Scrophularia vernalis
Yellow Iris	Iris pseudacorus
Yellow Loosestrife	Lysimachia vulgaris
Yellow Pimpernel	Lysimachia nemorum
Yellow Rattle	Rhinanthus angustifolius
Yellow Star-of-Bethlehem	Gagea lutea
Yellow Water Lily	Nuphar lutea
Yellow-horned Poppy	Glaucium flavum
Yew 'Dovastonii	Taxus baccata 'Dovastonii'

*The enchanted heemparks of
Amstelveen*

This publication was realised with
the assistance of: Eric Brandes,
Walter Busse, Henri Hennequin,
Rinus Hofs, Wil Melgers, Anthony
Reijersen van Buuren, Beate
Wesdorp, and Gerben Zeilinga.

AMSTELVEEN
FONDS

This walking guide to Amstelveen's
heemparks is published with support
from the Amstelveen Fonds.
The Amstelveen Fonds stimulates
and supports local initiatives with a
sustainable and socio-cultural
character that contribute to
maintaining and/or improving the
quality of life of Amstelveen's
residents.

http://wwwthijssepark.nl/
Check our website regularly for news
and additional information.

Scan the QR code with your smart-
phone to see our 'variety of the
month'.

Amstelveen

http://www.ivn.nl/amstelveen
We would like to draw your attention
to the free, guided tours in the
heemparks in Amstelveen. More
information about these is published
in the local newspapers and on our
website. Kindly contact us if you
would like a tour as part of a family
celebration or staff party. We charge
a fee for this service.

Stichting LM Publishers
Velperbuitensingel 8
6828 CT Arnhem
E-mail: info@lmpublishers.nl
www.lmpublishers.nl

©2014
Stichting LM Publishers-Arnhem

Original Dutch edition: *Dwalen
door betoverend heemgroen. Een
wandeling door de Amstelveense
heemparken De Braak, het
Dr. Koos Landwehrpark en het
Dr. Jac. P. Thijssepark*
(ISBN 978-94-6022-272-6)

TEXT:
Ariën Slagt and
Arlette Kouwenhoven
TRANSLATION:
Mark Poysden
PHOTOGRAPHY:
Thijssepark
Photographs on pp. 12, 20, 32 and 58
– Gemeente Amstelveen, assisted by
Stefan Toth (Amstelveenweb.com)
Image on p. 27 from Daniel Willink,
*Amstellandsche Arkadia, of
beschrijving van de gelegenheit,
toestant en gebeurtenissen van
Amstellandt....* (1773)
Photograph on p. 58 originally
Heimans en Thijsse Stichting
DESIGN:
Nel Punt, Weesp
PRODUCTION:
High Trade BV, Zwolle

ISBN 978-94-6022-273-3